TRAVELS IN THE

THE STORY OF JAMES EVANS

The Reverend James Evans

THE CREE

SYLLABIC CHARACTERS, TERMINATIONS, &c.

ā	e	o	ah	Terminations	Cree Terms with their meanings affixed, &c				
▽	△	▷	◁	ι p	L ḃ	But	Ρᑫ Lσↄ	The Great Spirit	
pa	pe	po	pah		Γ ᴀ	and again, or more	Lſ Lσↄ	The Evil Spirit	
V	∧	>	<	ı t.	Ρ ∧	river	ᴀ V°	A man.	
ta	te	to	tah		σ ∧	water	Δ∩Ρ°	A woman.	
U	∩	⊃	C	×ᴷ, ×K aspirated	Ρ ſ	duck	ᴀ VΡↄ	A boy	
kā	ke	ko	kah		σ Uᶜ	my horse	Δ·9·Ρↄ	A girl	
9	ρ	d	b	∩ s	ρ Uᶜ	your horse	◁◁·Ρↄ	An infant	
chā	che	cho	chah		DUL	his or her horse	J∩ↄ·	A buffalo	
?	ſ	J	b	>n	ρCΔ·	my father	J· ◁·	A moose	
mā	me	mo	mah		dCΔ'	your father	◁·◁·∩9 Ρↄ	A red deer	
⊓	Γ	J	L	c m	▷CΔ'd	his or her father	L∩b·	A bear	
nā	ne	no	nah		σd Ρ·	my son	◁Γↄ	A beaver	
Ό	σ	Ό	Ọ	-ch	Ρd Ρ·	your son	Ρ◊ Ρↄ	A fish	
sā	se	so	sah		▷d Ρↄ	his or her son	L9 Ρↄ	A fox	
4	Ρ	¿	5	•w *	◁∧	sit down	Ρ◊∧	A snake	
yā	ye	yo	yah		>Ρd	get up (from a seat)	∧≻·	A partridge	
∠	≻	?	7	°ew; °°wew	◁·Ⴇ·b	get up (from a bed)	◁J	A wasp.	
				≥ ℓ;ʒ r †					

* This, at the top of a character is equivalent to i, viz 9Ⴇ (kā-kwi). If the dot were not at the top, it would simply be kā-kwah.

† As there are no labials required for the language the above signs are used for ℓ and r when proper names are introduced: thus ⊓ʒΔ (Mary); <ε·(Pilate)

The Cree Syllabic alphabet.

TRAVELS IN THE
Shining Island

THE STORY OF JAMES EVANS AND THE INVENTION OF THE CREE SYLLABARY ALPHABET

Roger Burford Mason

Natural Heritage Books

Toronto

Travels in the Shining Island
by Roger Burford Mason

Published 1996 by Natural Heritage / Natural History
Inc.
P.O. Box 95, Station "O", Toronto, Ontario M4A 2M8

Printed and bound in Canada by Hignell Printing
Limited, Winnipeg, Manitoba
Designed by Steve Eby

Canadian Cataloguing in Publication Data
Burford Mason, Roger, 1943—
    Travels in the shining island
Includes bibliographical references and index.
ISBN 1-896219-16-0
1. Evans, James, 1801 - 1846. 2. Indians of North
America - Missions - Northwest, Canadian - History.
3. Methodist Church - Missions - Northwest, Canadian -
History. 4. Missionaries - Northwest, Canadian -
Biography. 5. Missionaries - England - Biography.
I. Title.
BV2813.E83B87   1996   266'.7'092   C96-931561-9

Natural Heritage / Natural History Inc. acknowledges
with gratitude the assistance of The Canada Council,
The Ontario Arts Council and The Association for the
Export of Canadian Books.

For Will Rueter,
and in memory of Marilyn Rueter,
book makers and book lovers,
who are both present in this book.

The cover of a prayer book, printed by Evans on buckskin in the syllabic alphabet he had recently developed. Norway House, 1841.

About the Author

Roger Burford Mason is editor of a Canadian trade magazine, and the author of several books and numerous newspaper and magazine articles. Until his arrival in Canada in 1988, he was well-known in British book art circles as the editor and publisher of *Albion*, the international journal of book history and the private press movement. *Albion* was produced from 1977 until Roger's move to Canada, and most university and college libraries subscribed to it, as well as most significant private press printers, bibliophiles and book scholars.

Married and a resident of Toronto, Roger Burford Mason is an ardent angler, whose love of sport fishing is only surpassed by his literary interests and activities.

UNUMEAGEESEG BUNUU-JEDOONG.

Ge-je-mu-ne-doo zu je-üun-gouu-me-nu-meng eoô u-nu-me-a-gee-seg; gees-ben dus da-boa-duu-ze-ouud e-geoô e-ne-ne-ong eoô guu-ë-ge-dood,

da buu-duu-ze-oug dus ge-duu-ë-ne ne-muu-nuu-neg, duu-bes-goo goo geoô oa-se-bee-oon-jeg o-muu o-ju-ee-ëe guu-bu-nuu-je-do'o-go-bua

SABBATH BREAKING.

God has commanded us to keep holy the Sabbath day, and when men refuse to keep his law, we may expect to see them come to some bad end, as those who are represented above, who,

A page spread from the Speller and Interpreter. *The illustrations are very much in the style of the 19th century wood-engraver, Thomas Bewick.*

Contents

"Birch bark talking." A pen and ink drawing by Toronto artist C.W. Jeffreys (1869-1951) of Evans teaching Indians his syllabics by inscribing then on a tree trunk.

Acknowledgments

$\int$OME PARTS OF THIS BOOK appeared first in *Albion*, the British quarterly of printing and publishing history now, alas, defunct. Other parts have appeared in *Applied Arts, Queen's Quarterly, Graphic Monthly, Bookways*, the US journal of the book arts, and in *The Printer*, a US publication devoted to printing history.

I would like to thank Linda White, Archival Assistant, The United Church of Canada, Archives - Conference of Manitoba and Northwestern Ontario, at the Rare Book Room Library at the University of Winnipeg, for providing information about Evans' death, burial in Hull, and reburial at Norway House. Few writers in Toronto can get by without the ministrations of the ever-helpful staff of the Metropolitan Toronto Reference Library, who found books, pamphlets and microfiches for me, usually on the basis of the scantiest information, and I am grateful for the help of the staff of the E.J. Pratt Library at the University of Victoria in Toronto, who led me to material I had only guessed that I needed.

I am indebted to my friend John Robert Colombo, who told me a long time ago that I should write this book, and then never forgot to remind me to do it. Also to Barry Penhale, this book's publisher, who has been an enthusiastic supporter of the book from the moment I took the idea to him. And finally, as always, to my wife Aileen, who has never been less than unstinting in her support of me, and for the most precious of all the gifts she has ever given me: time to write.

James Evans

Heroic Missionary

to the Indians of the

Great Lone Land.

LONDON:
C·H·Kelly,
2, Castle Street, City Road, E.C. & 66, Paternoster Row, E.C.

PRICE ONE PENNY.

Title-page of a late 19th century children's religious magazine.

Introduction

$\mathcal{I}$NVENTIONS THAT HAVE HELPED shaped human society are few indeed. The most famous case, perhaps, has become an axiom, "the best thing since the invention of the wheel." But one might canvas the domestication of fire, the discovery of magnetism or, in modern times, the invention of the microchip, which has put a computer in every spare bedroom, while each of us probably has made at least one liberating discovery of his or her own.

In my teenage years, when I learned to type and drive, my life was transformed by the acquisition of both skills. It was at this time also that I began to be interested in books and, more specifically, in the technology that went into producing them. Fifteen years later I acquired a small printing press myself and began, by laborious but enjoyable hand-work, to publish volumes of poetry, short stories and essays, and seriously to pursue the history of printing and publishing. It was then I realized that the discovery of printing by Johannes Gutenberg in Germany in the middle of the 15th century, must also have been one of those discoveries which revolutionized human society. "With twenty-six soldiers of lead," the unknown aphorist wrote, "I will conquer the world."

For centuries, monks in their scriptoria had created books and documents, some like the Irish *Book of Kells*, of astonishing complexity and beauty, which ordered and controlled the world the church dominated. Within the monasteries, the centres of learning of the time, their pens and paintbrushes recorded and decorated, in books which were slow and laborious to produce, the religion, laws, history, culture and administration of the whole known world. So rare were these books that most were locked in great libraries, with the rarest of all, chained to their shelves in the great 'chained libraries' of the monastic world, such as the one at Wimbourne Minister, in Dorset in the south of England.

In that early world, few people except monks and the clergy were educated enough to read. Indeed, it was an educated king or prince who could even write his own name. Fewer still had access to books and manuscripts which, at the time of the Normans' conquest of England in the 11th century, might have numbered, in generous terms, no more than a few thousand copies in the world altogether. The bulk of these would have been hand-copied copies of original works. Thus, the conflagration which destroys the monastery library at the end of Umberto Ecco's justly celebrated novel, *The Name of the Rose*, has no parallel in modern times which could illustrate to us just how much was lost when such a library was destroyed. The only modern image that might strike a similar chord would be to envisage the total destruction of the world's computer industry.

However, by the middle of the 15th century, the whole world of the monk-scribe began to disappear when a German goldsmith, Johannes Gutenberg, began improvising with the stamps he used to impress identification and validation marks on the items of gold he made. He realized that the same kinds of punch could be made for each of the letters of the alphabet and arranged into words, coated with ink and impressed on paper, over and over and over again. Here was the importance of printing; its enabling us to reproduce the same text quickly and in an unlimited number of copies. Printing democratized knowledge, history, culture and law. It put a Bible and a spelling book within the reach of every citizen. There could have been no mass education without the printed book. Imagine the effort involved in providing learning materials for a group of even twenty children if it all had to be produced by hand. As well, the whole history of the development and spread of general public education is closely tied to developments in the technology of printing.

Gutenberg's simple, hand-operated wooden printing press lasted until the Industrial Revolution before it gave way to more robust cast iron machines. These in turn gave way to presses operated by steam, and then by electricity, and now by the magic of the microchip. Each new development enabled more books to be produced, more quickly, in greater numbers.

In the 19th century Christian missionaries fanned out throughout the world to preach and teach. Their success or failure depended largely on how quickly they could introduce those they hoped to convert, to ideas presented to them with material printed in their own language. In most cases, both missionary teaching and evangelizing material were translated into native languages and printed in the Roman alphabets of the western world. It was the rare missionary who realized that Roman letters were not always best suited to the transliteration of the sounds of every language. For example, China and India already had many versions of their own very different forms of writing, while there were hundreds of native languages which had no form of written expression at all. This void was soon discovered by the first missionaries in North America as they tried to bring their message to the indigenous peoples.

I first heard of the 19th century Methodist missionary, James Evans, and his work in devising a written language for Canada's Ojibwa and Cree Indians, in Great Britain in the 1980s. At the time when I was editing and publishing *Albion*, a quarterly magazine about printing and publishing history. A subscriber in Canada sent me a brief note about Evans, suggesting that his story would make an interesting contribution to *Albion*. After some research in the archives of the British and Foreign Bible Society and the Methodist Church in Great Britain, I wrote a short article about Evans. I thought no more about it, not returning to the subject until I immigrated to Toronto in 1988. Here, nearer to the source, as it were, I did some more reading and research and fleshed out my *Albion* article into something more substantial, which was later published in *Queen's Quarterly*. It was my friend, the poet, author and anthologist, John Robert Colombo, who, knowing of my interest, as a printing historian, in Evans, suggested that it was time for another look at Evans' life. I thought so, too.

For a country of just thirty million people, and most of them newly arrived immigrants since 1900, Canada has not made as many contributions to the book arts as the more established nations of Europe. But two, at different historical periods, stand out as particularly distinguished contributions to the field of typography and the history of the book.

The most recent of the two was the work of Carl Dair, the internationally renowned typographer, book and print designer. His typeface, Cartier, designed in the 1960s, continues to be one of the most elegant typefaces in use for computer typesetting. As well, *Design for Type*, his most frequently cited book, stands with works by William Goudy, Stanley Morris and Beatrice Webb as among the most influential 20th century texts on book and printing design.

But even Dair's sterling work is overshadowed by the extraordinary achievement of James Evans. He not only developed a written script to transliterate the language of the Ojibwa and Cree Indians, but also was the first to print in the language of one of North America's indigenous peoples. Indeed, he was the first printer in Northern Canada.

Evans was born in 1800 into a Methodist family in the port city of Hull, on the east coast of England, but emigrated to Canada in 1820. Shortly afterwards he married Mary Blithe Smith and together they set up a mission to the Ojibwa Indians on behalf of the Canadian Methodist Conference at Rice Lake, near the modern city of Peterborough, Ontario.

It was during their work in this location that both James and Mary developed an abiding interest in Indian life and culture. In particular, through his semantic observations and research, James Evans developed a passion for systematizing the Indian languages along the lines of contemporary European philological thought.

It was when he was transferred to another mission near to the present-day Ontario town of Sarnia, that James Evans embarked upon his life's greatest work, studying the language of the Ojibwa to render it in a syllabic script. But it was not until another posting took Evans to the Hudson's Bay Company's fort at Norway House, some four hundred miles north of Winnipeg, that he began to frame plans for creating a form of type with which to print in the Indian languages.

Evans' spiritual task at this time was huge. His territory was unimaginably vast, covering all the settlements along the shores of Hudson's Bay, inland for many hundreds of miles and as far west as the Rocky Mountains. It required weeks of travel by dog-sled and canoe to visit the individual settlements of his flock. Furthermore, since the Cree followed their traditional nomadic life of fishing, hunting and gathering during the months of the year when it was possible, he had limited access to them. It was only at the times when their peregrinations brought them within the orbit of his mission or its outposts, or when he could glean intelligence of their whereabouts, and arrange to visit them in their temporary camps, that he could fulfill his calling.

Nevertheless, Evans travelled many thousands of miles every year to preach, teach and bring medical help to the Indians and, at the same time, study their customs and language. It was during these brief meetings that he began teaching them their own language in the characters he had invented.

This syllabic 'alphabet', devised by Evans to transliterate the Cree language as a script, was based upon a simple pattern of rotating shapes, not unlike a simplified shorthand. Though cumbersome to write by hand, Evans' Cree alphabet was robust and effective. In a few lessons, the majority of the Cree to whom he introduced it, written in soot and oil on birchbark, which the Cree called "the magic of the talking birchbark", had mastered it, and could read in their own language. Immediately, demand for texts in Cree outran Evans' ability to produce enough to satisfy his students. Each had to be written by hand by Evans, his wife, or by one of the Indian mission assistants. He quickly realized that to use his invention for the purpose he intended, that is, to propagate the faith through Bibles, prayer books, and hymnals whose texts the Cree could read, it would have to be cast in type and printed in multiple copies. Texts hand-written in the laborious fashion of the medieval scriptorium would never suffice.

At first, lacking typecasting equipment of any kind, Evans whittled crude matrices from wood and cast his characters in river clay, printing with them with a solution of soot, lamp oil and, sometimes, animal blood. But the characters he so painstakingly moulded proved too brittle for serious and prolonged use. He was at a loss to know how to proceed until he hit upon the solution of casting stronger and more durable characters using the thin sheets of lead foil that lined the Hudson's Bay Company's tea-chests. With large numbers of these in storage at the company's post nearby, he would have had a ready source of material.

Without a proper printing press, indeed, forbidden to acquire one for a number of years by the Hudson's Bay

Company for fear that a better educated Indian community would prove more difficult to deal with and control, Evans adapted a simple wooden press used to pack animal pelts for transportation as his printing press. He made his own ink and used paper from the mission supply. With these crude materials and his home-made type, he set and printed a variety of texts, some of which have survived and are in British archives in London. Some are with other papers and material, including his sketch books and diaries, in the Pratt Library at Victoria College in the University of Toronto.

In a diary entry for November 11, 1840, Evans writes:

My types answer well... I have got excellent type, considering the country and materials; they make at least a tolerably good impression. The letter or character I cut out in finely polished oak. I filed out one side of an inch square iron bar the square body of the type; and after placing the bar with the notch over the letter, I applied another polished bar to the face of the mould, and poured the lead in, after it had been repeatedly melted to harden it. These required a little dressing on the face and filing to the uniform square and length, but they answer well.

In a letter to his brother Ephraim in England, sent in June the following year from Upper Fort Garry on the Assiniboine River, Evans wrote seeking help in acquiring a press. He had, he wrote:

...made a fount of Indian type – press & nearly everything necessary, and beside making a nearly four month voyage, have printed about 5,000 pages in the Mushkego language. Among other things, a small volume of hymns... 100 copies, of 16 pages each.

It was not until Ephraim brought his brother's efforts to the attention of the English Weslyan Mission Society in London that he was able to consider formalizing his printing. With the grudging agreement of the Hudson's Bay Company, Evans was allowed to receive a cast-iron printing press and book-quality paper from the Wesleyan Mission Society in London. They had his syllabary type cast in metal for him in sufficient quantities to enable the production of more substantial work

With £500 also donated by the Wesleyans, Evans built a printing office at his Rossville Mission at Norway House. It was from there, bearing the imprint *Rossville Mission Press*, that the first bound books in the Cree language were issued.

The press's first publication was a version of the *St. John's* Gospel in a Cree translation by William Mason, another missionary, who was one of Evans' colleagues in the missions in the north-west. It was eight and a half inches by five inches, printed on fifty-three unnumbered pages (without a title-page), with ten verses on each page. It was followed by two further versions of *St. John*. One is bound in ticket-quality stock bearing the original imprint of the Weslyan Methodist Society's quarterly ticket for September 1846, while the other is distinguished by the addition of two rough woodcut illustrations by Evans.

Given the nature of the place where he printed and distributed his books, and the technology of the times, it is not surprising that little has survived of the *Rossville Press's* output from those years, but we may guess that it was more of the same. The last book from the press was *Certain Epistles*, published in 1857, eleven years after the first book was published, and eleven years also after Evans' death in England at the age of forty-six years. After that, all printing in the Cree syllabary type for the northern Canadian missions was undertaken in England by the Methodist Church. After taking over this work they issued their first Cree publication, the *Cree New Testament*, in 1859.

In good time, other churches engaged in missionary work among North America's first peoples came to hear about Evans' remarkable achievement. The British and Foreign Bible Society came to use the Cree syllabary type for hundreds of different publications sent to missions across the entire North American continent. Their variations allowed the printing of Inuit, Chippeway, Moose and many other Indian languages.

Today, versions of Evans' enduring alphabet are still in use in newspapers, magazines, notices, and ephemera published by and for Indian communities across Canada, as well as in many northern states in the United States. But the Roman alphabet of the majority culture is rapidly superseding it. Soon Evan's alphabet may be little more than a typographic and cultural curiosity, echoing the distant sounds of another time and another world. That it was created out of the perceived needs of that time and that world and served them well is all the more reason to accord Evans the place he has earned in the history of North America and its people.

Roger Burford Mason
Toronto, 1996

Chapter One

𝒯HE HUMBER RIVER, one of England's major waterways, flows down from the Yorkshire moors to meet the grey North Sea at a bleak and windswept estuary on the east coast, halfway between London and Edinburgh. A little inland from this confluence of land, river and sea, the old fishing port of Grimsby commands the south shore of the estuary while the town of Kingston-on-Hull, Hull to every English person, commands the north shore. One of the best of the metaphysical poets, Andrew Marvell, was a native of Hull. He returned there after the English Civil War and was drowned when the small boat in which he was crossing the Humber overturned.

It would have been, it probably still is, difficult to be born and grow up on the Humber estuary without some connection to boats and the sea. The area has produced both sailors and fishermen, as well as poets, explorers and saints. There were some elements of each in the life and work of James Evans.

Evans was born at Hull on January 18, 1801, the oldest of four children. His father, also James Evans, was the captain of a merchant vessel which traded in Europe, as far as the eastern end of the Baltic, and to the most exotic ports of call in the Pacific, the Caribbean and the China Sea.

Captain Evans was on business in the Baltic port of Kronstadt when his wife Mary gave birth to their first child, a son, at their substantial home, set back from the waterfront in Hull. The threat of Napoleon's ambition hung over all of Europe at that time. Nations which had every reason to fear the 'Little Corporal' were nervous. In the midst of this, Captain Evans plied his trade between his home port and the ports of the Baltic Sea. However, before he could return home to greet his first-born, he was captured and imprisoned by the Russian authorities. With his ship impounded to placate French demands that British activity in the Baltic be curtailed, he was not released until the weak and vacillating Czar Paul was overthrown. At that point, the embargo, which had prevented foreign merchants from trading in the Baltic, was lifted. As a result, before he could get back to Hull, Mary had had his new son baptized at the Carthruse Wesleyan Methodist Church in the town. She named him for his father. Hull was a bustling sea port and the young James grew up desperate for the day when he could follow his father to sea. Evans Senior, however, did not want his son to pursue a career as a sailor, for he could see that the day of the great sailing vessels was drawing to a close. Iron and steam were taking over from sail. With that development, he recognized that sailing would change from an exacting science and art into a tool of the mercantile system which was springing up in England and across Europe. Furthermore, Napoleon's looming presence, and the narrowness of the English Channel, made the sea a precarious choice of career at that time. On the other hand, Captain Evans knew his son's stubbornness well enough to know that a didactic ban would not achieve the required effect. Instead of discouraging him, therefore, he allowed the boy to sign on as a member of his own crew. James was nine years old when he sailed for the first time. His father gave him rough and difficult work to do and showed him no preference. James endured the hardship and disappointment for only two voyages, to Danzig, and to Copenhagen, and then decided to leave the sea and return to his studies.

With the outbreak of war, Captain Evans took command of a troopship, the *Triton*, and sailed to the Mediterranean, accompanied by his wife and two middle children. Left behind in England, James and his younger brother Ephraim were sent to a boarding school in Lincolnshire. There James would stay until he was fifteen.

But James was not a scholar at this point in his life, although his adult life would be dedicated to the pursuit of knowledge and would flower in a rigorous and ground-breaking study of North American Indian languages and cultures. He left school shortly after his fifteenth birthday and apprenticed to John Bryan, a grocer in Kingston. Bryan not only took him into his business but, as was common at that time, into his home as well. It was an important moment in James' life, for Bryan was an elder of the local Wesleyan church and he took young James there frequently.

It was at a Methodist chapel meeting one Sunday that James first heard the missionary, Gideon Ouseley, a famous Irish evangelist. He was greatly moved by the Irishman's passionate oratory and felt himself, in modern parlance, 'born again.' From that moment, the church claimed a major part in his life and he gave to it unstintingly. While still not much more than a boy, he became a lay-preacher, filling in for the minister when necessary, and preaching extemporarily wherever he could. In a short period of time the managers of the local Methodist Circuit recognized his earnestness and talent and soon elevated him to the rank of local preacher, the greatest honour a layman might achieve in the church.

When he was nineteen years old, James' family emigrated to Québec and settled at LaChute. Emigration was not immediately what James wanted to do with his life. Having a good command of languages and shorthand, he remained behind in England for two more years, working for a glass and crockery merchant in London. However, as he did not progress in the business as he would have wished, he finally set out for Québec to join his family once more.

One month after his arrival, he accepted a position as a school teacher at L'Orignal. It was a rough job for which he would require no training, only the ability to beat big boys into submission and maintain order in his classroom, while attempting to transfer some learning into the heads of his reluctant country pupils. While following revivalist preachers around in the English Midlands for several years, James had seen plenty of ruffianly behaviour. He was no stranger to the violent fisticuffs and cudgelling that had often erupted at open-air religious meetings, but he seemed to be a natural teacher who had little trouble in commanding the attention and respect of his students at the little school at L'Orignal.

It was while he was teaching there that he met Mary Blithe Smith. After courting briefly, they were married, although Mary's father initially objected. It was only Mary's telling him in no uncertain terms that unless she married James Evans, she would not marry at all, that settled the matter.

Two years later they moved west along the St. Lawrence River to the small community of Augusta. There, at a revivalist camp-meeting, James felt the call to enter missionary work. This was the era of frenzied missionary work by all the Christian churches in Canada. The time when Roman Catholics, Methodists, Moravians, Presbyterians and Baptists and others all vied with each other to save the souls of the Indians, not always to best effect. Many Indians rebuffed the overtures of the Christians, whom they saw, sometimes correctly, as drunks and fanatics.

The first efforts to make Christians of the Indians were made by Jacques Cartier and his followers in what is now Québec during the mid-16th century. His lead was followed assiduously by priests and missionaries from France, especially the Oblates and the Jesuits. They spread out through New France, and then on foot, by canoe, snowshoe or dog-sled, into the interior. They would reach as far north as the shores of Hudson's Bay, west to lakes Huron and Superior and thousands of miles into the lonely reaches of the north-west.

The Roman Catholics were followed by Protestant missions and, for one hundred and fifty years, the missionary struggle between Protestants and Catholics was as much a part of the national rivalry between France and England as it was a struggle for souls. Missions were at least as concerned with preventing 'their' people from going over to the other side as with winning them for the Christian God.

By the mid-18th century, missionary work had brought a rough patchwork of faiths to North America. Claiming various areas as their own, because they had been the first to take the Bible into those parts, the Roman Catholics, the English Protestants, the Dutch Reformed Church, the Moravian Brethren from Germany, the Congregationalists, the Baptists and the Methodists established missions among the Indians from the Florida Everglades as far north as the Arctic, and across both America and much of northern and north-western Canada. If some perished for their pains, others followed them unhesitatingly with a view to establishing a political claim to territory by collecting souls.

Missionary work grew in importance after the early 19th century, when it became fashionable in England and America to support missions overseas, including those in Canada. While

the Roman Catholic and Anglican churches, with their established orthodoxies, made the earliest headway among the Indians, the non-conformist churches were quickly competing successfully with them for converts among the Indians.

The evangelical revival which transformed England at this time, gave birth to missionary societies in most of the non-conformist churches. However, the Methodists were particularly adept at raising money for their missions by regular collections among the faithful. Although there was a long and drawn-out struggle for supremacy between the English and Canadian Methodist mission societies, it was largely played-out between the officers of each persuasion. Generally this power struggle did not effect the steady development of Methodist missions throughout Upper Canada and in the NorthWest.

In most of Upper Canada, Indians settled in any given place or area had the choice of at least two or three denominations of Christianity, but generally, the first church to set up its mission among them got the lion's share of the converts. Criticism was constantly being bandied about between the various missionary persuasions about 'tobacco converts', Indians who had been 'bought' for a particular faith by the generous application of bribes such as tobacco, trade goods and weapons. However, it should be recognized that many Indian bands weighed carefully the pros and cons of each denomination's spiritual and practical offerings before committing to one or the other.

The Anglicans and Roman Catholics, with a head start on the Methodists, had established the largest number of missions. Furthermore, each had already established its strengths in the eyes of the Indians, and those strengths were not inconsiderable. The Catholics were well received because although their brand of Christianity was very demanding, it was also very simple to absorb. As well, the Catholic missionaries, by living within their Indian communities, were on much more intimate terms with Indian life and customs. Of all the missionaries they were the best placed to observe and react to the pulse of Indian life and needs of the people.

Missionaries from all the Protestant and Non-Conformist churches lived at a greater remove than the Roman Catholics from 'their' Indians, generally in palisaded forts in exclusively

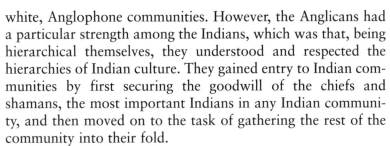

white, Anglophone communities. However, the Anglicans had a particular strength among the Indians, which was that, being hierarchical themselves, they understood and respected the hierarchies of Indian culture. They gained entry to Indian communities by first securing the goodwill of the chiefs and shamans, the most important Indians in any Indian community, and then moved on to the task of gathering the rest of the community into their fold.

The Methodists offered the hardest choice of all, for they demanded sudden and definite conversion of their converts, accompanied by a determined repudiation both of the past and of their Indian culture and spiritual traditions. But their own strength lay in the fact that, whereas other denominations distinguished socially between Indians and whites, Methodism called all men sinners equally and gave all the same hope of salvation. Methodism, with its aggressively democratic basis, appealed to the most impoverished Indian groups, especially those with a farming background.

Undoubtedly, the conversion of Indians was as much a political as a religious necessity, but if conversion brought the greatest benefits to the white colonisers, it also brought definite advantages to the Indians as well. A European kind of education was always seen as the key to long-lasting conversion. An Indian who could read the Bible and the prayerbook, and sing the hymns, was necessarily better educated and more susceptible than one who couldn't. But then, what started as a way of winning souls, was to become the faulty and inadequate mechanism through which the Indians had to confront the increasing numbers of white settlers and immigrants to their ancestral lands. Fragile as they were, the skills of reading and writing were among the few weapons the Indians were to have, small aid in a massive crisis, but better than nothing at all.

Along with the benefits of education, the missionaries brought European standards of cleanliness and health. Without a doubt, Christianity reduced the death rate among the Indians, especially among their children, because it taught that cleanliness was next to Godliness.

When he decided to answer the call to missionary work, Evans was fortunate to fall under the influence of one of the best missionaries in Canada, the Methodist, William Case, the Superintendent of the Canadian Conference of the Methodist church. Despite his winning rhetorical skills in the pulpit, Case was a shy man who felt more at home with Indians than with whites. He was singular among missionary leaders in seeing that native preachers would be important in winning over Indian converts. He encouraged a number of Indians to become missionaries in the Methodist cause, and trained and taught most of them himself. It was this charismatic man who persuaded James that his life's work lay in teaching Indian children.

"*Schools are very important everywhere among the Indians,*" James wrote to his brother Ephraim, who had been for some time comfortably ensconced as a Methodist pastor in the handsome town of Cobourg, on Lake Ontario between Toronto and Kingston. "*Beside the ordinary advantages of education, they form centres for devotion and religious instruction,*" he continued.

Two years later, James and Mary moved to Rice Lake, near the modern city of Peterborough. There James became a teacher at the school of the Ojibwa Indians of the Rice Lake Reserve. How different his life must have been from the comfortable town life of his brother in Cobourg can be surmised from a description of travelling in the Peterborough area, written by Catherine Parr Traill in her book, *The Backwoods of Canada*, published in 1836.

We soon lost sight entirely of the (Otonabee) *river, and struck into the deep solitude of the forest, where not a sound disturbed the almost awful stillness that reigned around us. Scarcely a leaf or bough was in motion, excepting at intervals we caught the sound of the breeze stirring the lofty heads of the pine-trees, and wakening a hoarse and mournful cadence. This, with the tapping of the red-headed and grey woodpeckers on the trunk of the decaying trees, or the shrill whistling cry of the little striped squirrel, called by the natives 'chitmunk,' was every sound that broke the stillness of the wild.*

Another English traveller of the period, Anna Jameson, can add texture to Traill's description with one of her own. Jameson, a well-known literary and art critic in the London of the early 19th century, travelled extensively in Canada with her husband. Her description of a carriage journey between the small south-western Ontario towns of Hamilton and Woodstock was published in *Winter Studies and Summer Rambles in Canada* in 1838. Here she catches what must have seemed like a forlorn emptiness in the wilderness which Europeans were only just beginning to tame and bring under the plough:

The seemingly interminable line of trees beyond you; the boundless wilderness around; the mysterious depths amid the multitudinous foliage, where foot of man hath never penetrated, - and which partial gleams of the noontide sun, now seen, now lost, lit up with a changeful, magical beauty—the wondrous splendour and novelty of the flowers, - the silence, unbroken but by the low cry of a bird, or hum of insect, or the splash and croak of some huge bull-frog,—the solitude in which we proceeded mile after mile, no human being, no human dwelling within sight...

Something of the quality of life for those intrepid early settlers can also be gleaned from a note by Ernest Thompson Seton (1860-1940), recorded in *Trail of an Artist-Naturalist*, published in the year of his death:

Quotidian ague, the doctor called it, or 'daily shakes' in folk tongue. It took us all in the same way; that is, each afternoon, at about three, we began to shiver and shake. It was impossible, even with the fire and the blankets, to give us any semblance of warmth.

From two til seven we had this deadly chill; then it would leave us. And from about seven until two next morning, we were in a raging fever. All we could do would be drink water and grow weaker. At two, the fever left us, and we lay feebly, snatching spells of sleep till sunrise.

According to Traill, the disease was endemic where the land was being cleared; *"...it arises from the exhalations of the vegetable soil, when opened out to the action of the sun and air."*

The Evans family did not escape their brush with it. From the St. Clair River Mission to which he was posted later, Evans wrote to his brother Ephraim in Cobourg about the effects of the plague at the mission:

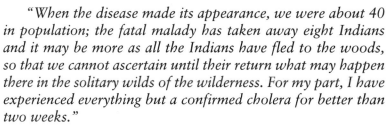

"When the disease made its appearance, we were about 40 in population; the fatal malady has taken away eight Indians and it may be more as all the Indians have fled to the woods, so that we cannot ascertain until their return what may happen there in the solitary wilds of the wilderness. For my part, I have experienced everything but a confirmed cholera for better than two weeks."

He tells his brother of suffering from severe dysentery himself, and of Mary's nausea and sickness although, he notes, *"Clarissa is a chip off the old block. She took her usual quantum of cake and butter and coffee for breakfast, which I hope will support her till dinner when I think she will repeat the dose."*

Despite, or perhaps because of, the hardships and trials of life in his distant mission post, James never complained of his lot. At the Rice Lake Reserve, he quickly became interested in the culture of the Indians. Soon he was speaking their language and finding ways to translate parts of the Scriptures into it.

The Indians were not without their own forms of written communication, although it was unlike any of the European scripts. It seems not to have been developed to record information or ideas permanently, like writing as it is understood in Europe. Early travellers in Canada had found that many of the Indian communities they met with could 'write', but only, as the Rev. Nathaniel Burwash noted in a paper he gave to the Royal Society of Canada in 1911, by using pictorial symbols *"...as a prompter to the memory of their old men."* Until the arrival of Europeans with their complex alphabets, the Indians could count and score, but seem to have had no means of putting more complex ideas into a written form. However, once they had started to master reading and writing, they proved quick studies. By 1828, Burwash observed, the Indians of Upper Canada had books, scripture, hymnals etc., written in their own Ojibwa language, in translations completed by the Indian pastor, Peter Jones and others. However, for many years their progress was hampered by the need to express the very different range of sounds contained in their language through the imperfect medium of the Roman alphabet. Nevertheless, Reverend Burwash claimed in 1911, at the time he was

9

speaking to the Royal Society of Canada, almost every Indian, *"...from the headwaters of the Ottawa River to the Rocky Mountains,"* could read in his own language. This he maintained, had not been achieved by mass formal education, but by the Indians themselves, spreading the skill by teaching one another, using bark and a charred stick where paper and pencil were not readily available.

Evans' strength, said Burwash, was that he had *"...a rare ear for languages, for their vocal music and their phonetic elements."* He was observant, alert to the information he received and inventive in finding ways to overcome barriers or problems. This trait would prove invaluable some years later when, needing a printing press, he found an ingenious way to make one, as we shall see.

When Evans entered missionary work, he encountered these early translations into the Ojibwa language; scripture, hymns and other short religious treatises done by earlier missionaries, as Burwash would much later report to the Royal Society of Canada. However, as Evans also correctly observed, such publications that existed used English orthography, which was only marginally useful in transliterating the very different sounds of the Indian language. In his work, Evans found that the ongoing problem lay in trying to teach the Indians both English and their own language, using the Roman alphabet. What worked perfectly well in the one, was confusing in the other.

Chapter Two

$\mathcal{T}$HE OJIBWA are among the most numerous of the native peoples of North America and certainly the largest single group in Canada. When the first white men began to penetrate their ancestral lands in the early 17th century, it is estimated that there were probably thirty-five thousand Ojibwa spread throughout the forests of south-west and south-east Canada, and the northern states of America. The word for their name means 'puckered up', referring to the way they stitched their moccasinsi They, however, called themselves the Anishi-nabe, meaning 'the people' or 'the first people'. However, the Ojibwa around the present city of Sault Ste Marie were usually called the Saulteur or Salteaux, the name the early French explorers of the area gave the Indians they met, because they were 'the people of the rapids'.

With allowances for regional variation, the Ojibwa generally lived in villages of conical or dome-shaped wigwams of birchbark, or of cattail mats on a pole frame. In addition, there would be one or more small conical sweat lodges for treating the sick or for ceremonial purposes. Theirs was a clan-based society, with clans named for the desirable characteristics of birds and animals, with moose, loon and bear being popular clan designations.

In the summer, the Indians lived a communal village life, farming corn, beans, squash, tobacco and pumpkin, as well as fishing with nets, bone hooks or spears. At night they used birchbark torches, which they shone from their canoes, to attract fish to their spears or nets. They entertained themselves with games such as snow-snake and lacrosse, or by gambling with flat-sided wooden dice which were coloured differently on each side. They tossed these in the air and caught them in a wooden bowl, and won or lost by their ability to predict which colours would fall into the bowl face-up. At set times during the year they would gather for a 'midewewin', or clan gathering, at which new medicine men would be initiated. Several writers have described the famous clan gatherings at what is

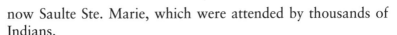

now Saulte Ste. Marie, which were attended by thousands of Indians.

In winter the villages broke up again and individual families, or small groups of related families, went their ways to their hunting grounds. There they would hunt for deer, moose, lynx, marten, rabbit, beaver or otter, (and caribou in northern areas). They used the bow and arrow, of course, but also snares, such as the 'babiche', made of sinew attached to a bent sapling, or a deadfall, a cleverly balanced log which would fall and stun the beast when it took bait from beneath it. In addition, they foraged for food from the wild, for berries, roots, shoots, nettles, eggs and nuts.

Their hunting grounds would typically cover hundreds of square miles of territory, within which they would usually overlap with other Indians. When a big kill was made, a moose or an elk perhaps, everything would be moved to the site. Camp would be pitched there while the meat was cut, treated and made into pemmican for the winter and for consumption on long journeys. Such was the mobility of an Ojibwa family that everything they owned would weigh less than a moose. Perhaps that is why it was less work to pitch camp beside the kill than to transport the kill back to the camp.

The Ojibwa had a mystical relationship with the natural world and a complex and highly-developed religion which ministered to it. They believed in 'manitos', or spirits, which resided in all things, animate or inanimate, and they acknowledged 'Gitche Manito' as 'the great spirit'. Their shamans were the wise people of the band. Shamans conducted ceremonies, had visions and made predictions, and cured the sick. James Evans was one of the few missionaries who made the effort to understand and empathize with the Indians' belief system. It was one of the qualities which made him so successful in his work among the Ojibwa and, later among their cousins, the Cree of the northern forests.

The Ojibwa language is a branch of Algonkian, in which very long strings of sound, akin to the European sentence, are put together to form compound words, not unlike the way German is constructed. Evans studied the sounds of Ojibwa and developed a system of writing which used individual

Roman letters to represent each voiced syllable of the language he was hearing.

He found that the sounds of the language could be best rendered by the consonants b, d, g, j, m, n, s and z. The vowels a, e, o and u, could be used as perfect vowel sounds. He doubled the vowels—aa, oo, uu—to represent the long sound of these vowels, maintaining each sound as a perfect vowel sound.

This was a significant improvement on what had been obtained previously, which had been a system of spelling Indian 'words' phonetically, using standard English orthography. However, Evans quickly perceived, and this was his important breakthrough, that he might create symbols, uniquely different from Roman characters, which would represent whole voicings, or sounds, from which the representation of meaning in Ojibwa could be built. For example, in the system he began to develop, the symbol < represented the sound 'pa', a common enough sound in Ojibwa. Then if < sounded 'pa', << made the word 'papa'. In Evans' system there were nine basic sounds, a, p, t, k, ch, m, n, s, and y; and four positions for the vowel which accompanied them, facing right, left, up or down. Thus, any sound could be rendered by choosing the basic sound shape and then rotating it through 90 degrees to achieve different vowel sounds. This is illustrated through an alphabet and its use in printing *Psalm One Hundred* (see illustration on page 17.)

What began at Rice Lake was continued at every other mission in Upper Canada to which Evans was posted. But it took years of what he described as 'attentive investigation' before he developed an independent syllabary alphabet which included all the sounds and sound groups of the Ojibwa language.

But those developments were still to come. In the meantime, the Evans' situation at Rice Lake was very difficult and he and his family undoubtedly suffered great hardships in pursuing their work. On one occasion he had written to Case to ask for supplies, and must have been disheartened to receive the reply, *"Funds for Rice Lake are scanty, and for the present we must live within our means. We sent you twelve yards of cotton that will answer for a feather bed, and I will send you some writing quills."*

Evans and his wife were not alone in their hardships. For most of the settlers trying to clear land and create a new life for themselves in the hinterland of Lake Ontario, breaking the land on an Upper Canada farm was demanding. In his essay, "On the margins of empire" in *The Illustrated History of Canada*, Graeme Wynn quotes from a letter by an Irish immigrant: *"My time at home is occupied in shoeing horses, making gates, chimney pieces, and furniture. Indeed my mechanical labours are so multifarious that I can hardly enumerate them, but you may form some idea of their versatility when I tell you that I made an ivory tooth for a very nice girl and an iron one for a harrow within the same day."*

Even so, the Evans' hardship was often extreme. A contemporary at Rice Lake wrote of visiting the Evans at their home, where he found them *"...without anything to eat save a little flour. To render this more palatable and nutritious, as they thought, it was mixed with fish spawn and eaten like pancakes; which was partaken of not only with resignation but with gratitude and cheerfulness. James Evans was literally a man who made a sport of hardship and privation."*

The hardship, and the prejudices too, of the early white settlers are well illustrated in an anecdote told by Nila Reynolds in her excellent history of the Haliburton Highlands, *In Quest of Yesterday*. Some time in the middle 1800s, Esther Austin, the wife of a fur trapper and trader, Willett C. Austin, was alone in her isolated home beside Stewart's Narrows, where Head Lake flows into Grass Lake just north-east of the town of Minden. Her husband had taken his furs in a flat-bottomed boat to sell at the auction in Peterborough, prior to buying supplies and provisions.

Esther knew nothing about the Indians she sometimes saw in their canoes as they passed through the narrows and, like most settler-women of her period, she was mortally afraid of them, although she had never had a personal encounter with one. One morning she was taking a batch of freshly-baked loaves out of her oven when a noise made her turn round in time to see an Indian walk into her kitchen, take a still-warm loaf off the table, and walk out without a word.

When her husband returned, she gave him a tongue-lashing for exposing her to such danger and could not be mollified, despite his assurances that all the Indians in the district were

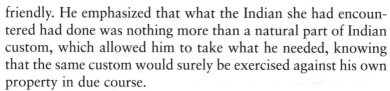

friendly. He emphasized that what the Indian she had encountered had done was nothing more than a natural part of Indian custom, which allowed him to take what he needed, knowing that the same custom would surely be exercised against his own property in due course.

Some time later, Esther Austin found herself alone again as her husband was away from home and not expected to return for a long period of time. On this occasion, with her supplies all but exhausted and replenishments not expected until her husband's return, Esther cooked the last of the venison she had in her store-cupboard, aware that there were no neighbours near enough to go to for help and nothing in the house left to eat. As she was considering what to do, the same Indian with whom she had had her frightened encounter, stepped impassively into her kitchen with a haunch of freshly killed deer over his shoulder. He put it down on the table, bowed to her and passed back out into the forest, his debt repaid. From that moment, Esther Austin became one of the most passionate and vocal spokespeople for the Indians of the district. She lost no opportunities to meet, know and understand them.

At Rice Lake, the Evans family lived in a tent while James built a house, a school and a church with the help of his Indian neighbours. Within the year, he had more than forty Indian pupils attending the school, of whom, he noted, twenty-one could already read the Bible, their only textbook, in English. To help the Indian community practically as well as spiritually, Evans found a ready and profitable market in the towns of Kingston, York (now Toronto), Peterborough and Cobourg for the baskets, axe handles, wooden scoops, shovels and brooms the Indian adults made when they were not hunting or tending their fields. It was the kind of practical application of faith which distinguished Evans from many of his contemporaries, and generally made him more acceptable to the Indians among whom he lived and worked.

In 1830, after nearly ten years serving as a mission teacher to the Indians and in other lay capacities in his church, James was received into the Methodist ministry at Kingston. He was sent as minister to the Rice Lake and Mud Lake Indians, taking charge of the Cavendish Circuit and its seventeen appoint-

15

ments before the year was out. Now *"circuit-rider"* was added to the host of his other duties.

In the early days of Methodism in Upper Canada, the circuit riders, or saddlebag preachers, covered many hundreds of miles, alone, in largely unknown and sparsely inhabited territory, taking services to distant homesteads and settler communities. That it was an eventful life is borne out by a note recorded by one such saddlebag preacher, who wrote of being tossed from his horse while travelling in the back country, north of the present city of Peterborough. *"I soon found myself in one place,"* he noted wryly, *"my horse in another, and my umbrella some distance from both of us."* Elsewhere, of his itinerant life he observed, *"My saddle was my study. My saddlebags my wardrobe, and my Bible and my hymn book my select library. I had no place to call home, yet I found home wherever night overtook me."*

In her history of the Haliburton Highlands, Reynolds records something of the life of a circuit-riding minister, describing a way of life with which Evans would have become wearily familiar. In the early 1860s, the Rev. George Henry was sent to the newly-established mission at Gull River, near Minden. The records in the United Church archives show that he led three services on the Sunday of his first weekend at the mission; at 10:30 a.m. at Gull River; at 2:30 p.m. at the home of a settler some six miles away; and at 7:30 p.m. back at the Gull River Mission. Preserving Henry's own idiosyncratic English, Reynolds quotes from a typical weekend itinerary of his mission work:

On Saturday I started out and took dinner at Hunter's at Burnt River (now the village of Kinmount) *and arrived at Mr. Peck's about 3 in the afternoon. My morning appointment was about six miles in the rear of Mr. Peck's. There was no road to get to it, a road had been cut through the underwood, but the logs had not been cut out, there was a rapid river to be crossed, and there was no bridge and no bridges over the bogs and swamps and these were not frozen up, and the only guide as to the course to take was the tracks of two men who had come through several days before and their tracks were nearly obliterated by freshly fallen snow. Mr. Peck tried to dissuade me from attempting to go through especially as the afternoon was near gone, but stay with them. I was very anxious to get through especially as this was my first time. I thanked him and said if he would keep my horse I would make the attempt, this he kindly consented to do, and I immediately set out. It was very hard walking, the snow being about a foot deep and some places there were several inches of mud under the snow...*

To Evans, who had lived in a tent in the winter and eaten flour and fish-roe pancakes, riding the circuit could not have been anything more than yet another difficult, but not insurmountable, test of his faith.

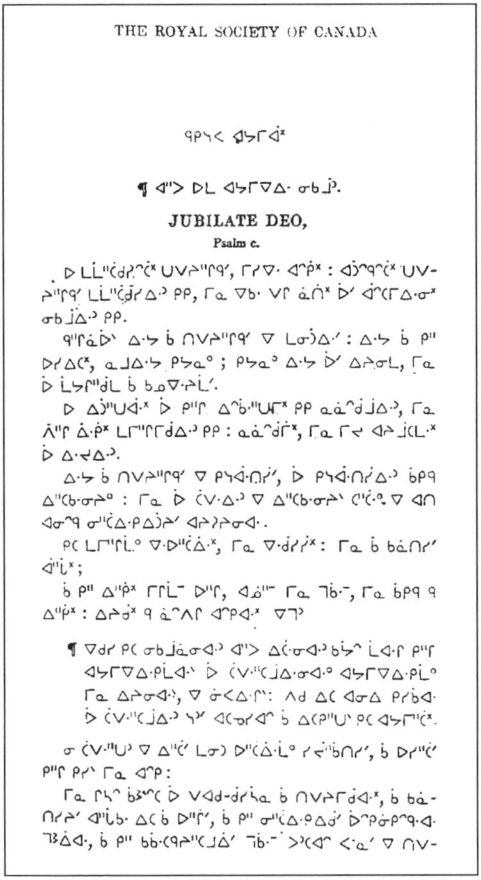

THE ROYAL SOCIETY OF CANADA

ᑫᑊᐦᐸ< ᐊᐺᒐᐧᑯᕁ

¶ ᐊᐻᕐ ᗡᒪ ᐊᐺᒉᐁᐧ· ᓄᑫ᛫ᒎᐦ.

JUBILATE DEO,

Psalm c.

ᗡ ᒪᒣᐦᐨᑯᕐᒣᐨ ᑫᐺ᛫ᐦᕐᑫᐧ, ᒥᕐᐁ· ᐊᐧᐳᕁ : ᐊᐧᐧᒐ᛫ᐨ ᑫᐺ᛫ᐦ᛫ᐦᐦᑫᐧ ᒪᒣᐦᐧᑯᑦ ᐁᐧᐧ ᑉᑉ, ᒐᐧ ᐁᐺᐧ· ᐁᕐ ᐋᐧᑎᕁ ᗡᐧ ᐊᐨᒐᐁ·ᐧᕁ ᓄᑫ᛫ᒎᐧᐧ ᑉᑉ.

ᑫᐧᒉᐋᗕᐧ ᐁᐺᕐ ᒍ ᑕᐺᐦᑫᐧ ᐁ ᒍᐧᐋᐁᐧ· : ᐁᐺᕐ ᒍ ᑉᐦ ᗞᐧᐊᐨᑦ, ᐊᐧᒍᐁᐺᕐ ᑉᐺᐧᐨ ; ᑉᐺᐧᐧ ᐁᐺᕐ ᗡᐧ ᐁᐺᐺᒪ, ᒐᐧ ᗞ ᒫᐺᐦᑯ·ᒪ ᒍ ᗞᐧᐁᐧ·ᐦᒪᐧ.

ᗡ ᐁᐨᐧᐧᑌᐧᐦᕁ ᗞ ᑉᐦᒐ ᐁᐧᐦᐧ·ᐦᐳᕐᕁ ᑉᑉ ᐊᐧᐨᐨᐧᒍᐁᐧᐧ, ᒐᐧ ᐧᐦᕐᒣ ᐋᐧᑉᕁ ᒪᕐᐦᒥᒉᐊᐧᐧ ᑉᑉ : ᐊᐧᐨᐺᕐᕁ, ᒐᐧ ᒥᐧᐧ ᐊᐺᐦᒎᒪ᛫ᕁ ᗞ ᐁ·ᐺᐊᐧ·ᐧ.

ᐁᐺᕐ ᒍ ᑕᐺᐦᑫᐧ ᐁ ᑉᐧᐊ·ᑎᕐᐧ, ᗞ ᑉᐧᐊ·ᑎᕐᐁᐧᐧ ᑉᑉᑫ ᐁᐦᐨᑉ·ᓄᐳᐧ : ᒐᐧ ᗞ ᐨᐺ·ᐁ·ᐧ ᐁᐦᐨᑉ·ᓄᐳᑦ ᐨᐧᐦᐧ· ᐁ ᐊᑎ ᐊᓄᐧᒐ ᓄᐨᐺᑕᑯᐁᐳᐺᐧ ᐊᕐᐧᐺᓄᐊᐧ·.

ᑉᐨ ᒪᕐᐦᒥᐦᐦᐋᐧ ᐁᐧᐦᐦᐨᐊᐧᕁ, ᒐᐧ ᐁᐧᐧᒥᒥᕁ : ᒐᐧ ᑉ ᑉᐋᐧᒎᕐ ᐊᐦᐨᐺᕁ ;

ᑉ ᑉᐦ ᐁᐦᐳᕁ ᒥᒥᒪᐧ ᗡᐦᒥ, ᐊᐧᐋᐦᐧ ᒐᐧ ᐦᑉ᛫ᐧ, ᒐᐧ ᑉᑉᑫ ᑫ ᐁᐦᐳᕁ : ᐁᐺᐧᐺ ᑫ ᐋᐦᐦᐋᒥ ᐊᐨᑉᐊᕁ ᐺᐨᐺ

¶ ᐺᐧᐧ ᑉᐨ ᓄᑫ᛫ᒎᐦᐊᐧᐧ ᐊᐻᐺ ᐊᐨᐺᐊᐧᐧᐺᐦᕁ ᒫᐊᕐ ᑉᐦᒥ ᐊᐺᒉᐁᐧ·ᑉᒪᐊᕁ ᗞ ᐨᐺ·ᐦᐨᒎᐧᐺᐊᐧᐧ·ᐁᐧ ᐊᐺᒉᐁᐧ·ᑉᒪᐧ ᒐᐧ ᐊᐺᐊᐧᐦᐦᐧ, ᐺ ᐧᐺᐨᐧ·ᒣ : ᐁᑦ ᐊᑦ ᐊᐦᒐ ᑉᕐᐺᐧ· ᗞ ᐨᐺ·ᐦᐨᒎᐧᐺᐧ ᐦᕁ ᐊᐨᐺᐨᐺᕁ ᑉ ᐊᐨᑉᐦᐺᕁ ᑉᐨ ᐊᐺᒐᐧᕐᐦᐨᕁ.

ᓄ ᐨᐺ·ᐦᐺᐧ ᐺ ᐊᐦᐨ ᒣᐧ ᗡᐦᐧᐋᐧᐺᐦᒍᐧ ᒥᐨᐺᐦᐺᓄᒣᐧ, ᑉ ᗡᒥᐦᐨ ᑉᐦᒥ ᑉᒥᐧ ᒐᐧ ᐊᐦᑉ :

ᒐᐧ ᒥᐺᐧ ᐁᐺ᛫᛫ᐨ ᗞ ᐺᐊᐧᐨ-ᐊᕐᐺᐧ ᑉ ᑕᐺᐺᒥᐊᐧᐧᕁ, ᑉ ᑉᐋᐧᐺᐺᕐᐧᐁᐧ ᐊᐧ᛫ᐺᐧ· ᐊᐨ ᑉ ᗡᐦᒥᕁ, ᑉ ᑉᐦ ᓄᐦᐧᐺᐧ·ᐺᐊᐧᐧ ᗡᐧᐺᐧᐺᐊᐧ·ᐧᐊ· ᐦᑕᐋᐧ, ᑉ ᑉᐦ ᐺᐺ·ᐨᑫᐺᐧᐦᐨᒎᐺᐧ ᐦᑉ·ᐧ ᐧᐺᑦᐺᐧ ᐺᐧᐋᐧ ᐺ ᑕᐺ-

The Jubilate Deo, part of the One Hundredth Psalm, in Cree Syllabics.

17

Chapter Three

WILLIAM CASE returned from a lecture and fund-raising tour in the United States with sufficient money to begin translating and publishing the Scriptures in the Ojibwa language. This endeavour he put in the hands of James Evans, Thomas Hurlburt and Peter Jones, a missionary who was to be a recurring figure in Evans' life and work.

Jones was the illegitimate son of a Mississauga Indian woman and one Augustus Jones, a Welshman who was a British government surveyor. Jones' Indian name was Kak-ke-Wa-Quo-Na-By, or Sacred Eagle. He, with his sister, Mary, had been among the first converts of the American evangelist, Alvin Torry, at the Grand River Reserve of the Six Nations, in southern Ontario, the site of the first Methodist Indian Mission in Canada. Like Evans, Jones had experienced a sudden and unexpected conversion at a camp meeting, which gave Case and the Methodists the entry they needed into the culture and communities of the Mississauga Indians. This group was a branch of the Ojibwa, but among the poorest, the least progressive and most superstitious of all the Indians in Upper Canada.

Methodism quickly spread from its spawning ground near Ancaster throughout the settlements of the Lake Ontario shore. It was not by the conscious efforts of the missionaries, although they did what they could to hasten its spread, but largely because of the intermingling of the Ojibwa people, who carried what they learned from one community to another. In a short time Methodism was established at the town of Belleville, between York (Toronto) and Kingston. From there it was taken north to the area around Rice Lake, where Evans was sent to propagate and develop it among the Indians. In a short period of time, five reserves had been organized by the Methodist missions for its Indian converts in the Rice Lake area, with Ojibwa from ten different bands at the five reserves. There were now, in the area, sixteen schools, employing seventeen missionaries, of whom nine were Ojibwa. Case wrote to Evans, *"We are much pleased with the specimens of writing of the children at*

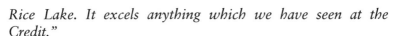

Rice Lake. It excels anything which we have seen at the Credit."

When Peter Jones received a letter from Evans in Ojibwa, he remarked that it was, *"...the first letter in the Indian language written by a white man that I have seen. There were but a few mistakes to be found."*

Case was keen for Evans to teach his Ojibwa alphabet to Indians throughout the area. *"Jump in my sleigh,"* he wrote to Evans, *"and spend but one week with them... I believe you would do better than any other person we have. I wish you to prepare drawings for their schools, taken from the patterns you have, with the improvements you have made."*

In 1831, in order to spread Evans' new orthography among a wider base of users, Case sent him to the mission at the Credit River, just west of the present-day city of Mississauga. The Mississauga Indian village at the Credit was one of the showplaces of the Methodist missions. It had been reorganized in 1826 as a 'model' village, with a church, a school and European-style houses. Now it was governed by the Methodists' aim for 'their' Indians to be educated and trained so that they would, *"...extend the knowledge of God, of learning, and of agriculture and Mechanism."*

Evans continued his translation work there, as well as working with the Indians and serving as pastor to the white settlements close by. While Evans was at the Credit, Case wrote to him, urging him to work faster on his translations: *"...it would be a very great advantage to all of us in acquiring a knowledge of the language to have a vocabulary of Indian words and their meaning in English. Hasten to it, Brother, as fast as your means will allow."*

However, despite the urgent need argued by Case for Evans to pursue his work with the Ojibwa language, he was not left to settle for long in any one place. Constantly he was moved from one posting to another. So it was that the next year, 1832, he was sent to Ancaster, near Hamilton, as missionary-in-charge. A year later he was a fully ordained minister and was stationed at St. Catharine's.

As a teacher, Evans differed significantly from his contemporaries in that he realized that whatever the Indians were taught had to be adapted to the lives they were going to live as adults. What was suitable for the white people would not satisfy their needs. He built his teaching on this perception and was not only more successful than most other missionaries, but better liked and respected.

But the Evans' family continued to be poor. James wrote jokingly to his brother in Cobourg, "*If we have a single sixpence for the postage, you will get this* (letter)," adding as an afterthought, "*Mary joins me in all but postage.*"

By this time, James and Mary had a child, a daughter Clarissa Eugenia, on whom Evans doted as his 'dear little Sparebones.' She grew up in her family home alongside Indian children and with a succession of orphans and invalids who found temporary shelter in her parents' house. Her closest friend was Julia Ann Southwind, the daughter of an Indian chief from Rice Lake, who wanted a proper education for his daughter. Julia Ann and Clarissa Eugenia were as close as natural sisters and shared Evans as a teacher:

"*Clarissa and Ann are learning pretty well,*" Evans wrote to his mother in Québec. "*They read distinctly from the Testament. Clarissa understands a great deal of Indian, and Mary speaks* (it) *among the women.*"

From St. Catharine's, James was sent to the mission at the St. Clair River, near the present town of Sarnia. This was a dangerous and difficult posting because the Indians there were more resistant to the missionary gospel than many of the other Indians of the region. But Evans, fluent enough in their language and empathetic to their culture, brought about a change of heart in them. Succeeding generations of missionaries at the St. Clair Rapids mission would comment on and benefit from this alteration. In addition to his work among his own Indian community, Evans also crossed the St. Clair River to preach and teach among the Indians in Michigan, on the American side. His popularity among them all arose from his lack of censoriousness about their behaviour and customs. He was also singular among white people, and especially among missionaries, in interesting himself uncritically in the religion of the Indians. He saw them not as pagans, but as people devout in the practice of their own faith.

Jonathan Carver (1710-1780) published a record of his own travels in northern Ontario in 1778. *Travels through the Interior Parts of North America in the years 1766, 1767 and 1768* contains an interesting account of the kind of spiritual beliefs Evans would have encountered in his own travels and teaching. Carver travelled around the north shore of Lake Superior in 1776, where he became fascinated by the legend of the golden sand:

One of the Chipeway (Ojibwa) *chiefs told me, that some of these people being once driven on the island of Mauropas* (now called Michipicoten Island) ... *found on it large quantities of heavy shiny yellow sand, that from their descriptions must have been gold dust. Being struck with the beautiful appearance of it, in the morning, when they re-entered their canoe, they attempted to bring some away; but a spirit of amazing size, according to their account more than sixty feet in height, strode into the water after them, and commanded them to deliver back what they had taken away. Terrified at his gigantic stature, and seeing that he had nearly overtaken them, they were glad to restore their shining treasure; on which they were suffered to depart without further molestation. Since this incident, no Indian that has ever heard of it will venture near the same haunted coast. Besides this, they recounted to me many other stories of these islands, equally fabulous.*

Such superstition and idolatry were inimical to most missionaries and they sought to stamp out every vestige of pagan belief and custom among the Indians. Evans no doubt made himself unpopular by pointing out the hypocrisy of the white missionaries who, for example, denounced the Indians for wearing amulets and charms to ward off evil spirits, while not questioning the motives of white people who carried lucky coins or holy medals. He sympathized openly with them when they were accused of being too enthusiastic in their worship, noting in a letter to his brother that many white Christians complained of the Indians "...*because they will praise the God of their salvation and make too much noise for their (the white people's) refined notions of order and decorum.*"

That summer at St. Clair Rapids, Evans made a missionary tour of Lake Huron, including a visit with a government expedition to distribute government goods to the Indians at Manitoulin Island in Georgian Bay. There he saw a treaty signed between the Indians and the government officials and witnessed a war-dance. This new experience impressed him deeply and intensified his interest in this strange and magnificent culture.

Evans' interest in the philology of the Ojibwa language was heightened during his time at the St. Clair River Mission. From his careful study of the Ojibwa language, he realized that a mere eight consonants and four vowels (he would later add 'y' to the mix) could render this entire language, whose voicing was so different from the sound of any European language. This discovery formed the basis of a new way of transliterating the sound of the Ojibwa language in the form of a syllabic alphabet developed by Evans. The same alphabet was used in some of the translations that he and his colleagues were working on at the time.

However, unfortunately for Evans, the British and Foreign Bible Society was engaged in printing religious material for the Indians using the Roman alphabet. Not wanting the distraction of Evans' syllabics, they tried to put a halt to the development of his new system. Consequently, Evans directed his attention to improving the approved alphabet-based version of Ojibwa. The result was his *Speller and Interpreter in English and Indian* (see page vi) which, though it used the English alphabet, was a great improvement over anything that was currently available. This, however, was not yet fully satisfactory, for it still left the student, learning to read and write in both English and their own Ojibwa language, confused by the different values of the same character in each language. Nevertheless, later, when Evans was sent to the northernmost limits of European exploration among the Cree of Northern Manitoba, the system upon which he had been working for so long was to become the building blocks of an entirely new way of printing in an Indian language.

Meanwhile, the translating work was nearing completion and in 1837 Evans was sent to New York to see the translations through the press. With characteristically little financial help from the Methodist missions, it was work done under the most exacting circumstances of personal hardship.

He journeyed to New York by stagecoach and riverboat. Of his life aboard the boat he wrote to Mary, "*I took passage and slept three nights on the softest plank I could find...*" and continued that he had told the other passengers, many of whom he was surprised to find he knew, that he was travelling cheaply to save money for his stay in New York: "*I told them all I was a deck-passenger feasting on my wife's excellent lunch basket, and I didn't give a sou...*"

In New York, Evans met Peter Jones, the Indian missionary with whom he had worked extensively in the past, and would continue to work in the future. Jones was on his way to England. There he would impress everyone with his handsome good looks, his gilded tongue and charms, and his quick and lively mind. He would be fêted throughout London society as that exotic thing, an 'educated Indian', and introduced at court, where he would meet and converse with Queen Victoria.

Writing to his wife from New York, Evans noted: "*My spelling book has cost me $151 and a few cents printing; the hymns, $554.91, and the music $1,000, all of which, with my little bill of expense here and travelling, will exceed a York six-pence. I'm as poor as a church mouse... I was seven or eight weeks with not twenty-five cents to spend. But I am as fat as a beaver, and as nimble as a deer...*" As a postscript he added, "*You must keep a good fire as I shall be coming creeping in some evening very cold.*"

It was a very prescient remark for the winter was early and harsh and he only got home at all by building a raft of lumber, bought on credit. Poling it through the thick ice on the St. Clair River to his home at the mission at the St. Clair Rapids was more than just numbing experience.

Nevertheless, he returned to Canada from New York with physical proof of his strenuous and self-denying efforts. With him were printed portions of the Bible to use as readers, as well as copies of psalms and hymns. In addition, he had boxes full of copies of his *Speller and Interpreter in English and Indian*, which provided a glossary of words in Ojibwa, side by side with their meanings in English. The *Speller*, printed for him in New York by D. Fanshaw, printer, at 150 Nassau Street, was sent immediately to England for approval by the British and

Foreign Bible Society. Evans was devastated when word returned in mid-summer 1838 that it had been rejected and would not be sanctioned for use because it was insufficiently 'limpid', clear or transparent, according to the Oxford dictionary, for general use.

In a pattern with which he and his family were wearily familiar, almost immediately on his return to Canada, Evans and another missionary, Thomas Hurlburt, were reposted. This time they were sent to the area around Lake Superior in 1838, the year of the rebellion in Lower Canada. They were to replace Peter Jones, now back from his successful visit to London, and another Indian preacher, John Sunday

If the missions at Rice Lake, the Credit and the St. Clair River were difficult postings, the Lake Superior missions were at the lonely, harsh fringes of European society. In her travels, Anna Jameson journeyed by canoe on Lake Superior, from Mackinaw Island to Saulte Ste. Marie, in the company of Mrs. Schoolcraft, the Indian wife of the American agent on Mackinaw Island. Of that journey she wrote:

All was so solitary... two days and nights the solitude was unbroken; not a trace of social life, not a human being, not a canoe, not even a deserted wigwam, met our view. Our little boat held on its way over the placid lake and among green tufted islands; and we its inmates, two women, differing in clime, nation, complexion, strangers to each other but a few days ago, might have fancied ourselves alone in a new-born world.

Characteristically, Evans sent Hurlburt, his assistant, to the relatively comfortable permanent posting at Fort William (the modern city of Thunder Bay). He assigned himself to travel between, and live among, the remote Indian bands encamped along the north shore of Lake Superior.

The work of the two men was similar: teaching, preaching and gaining converts. But where for the next two years, Evans' life was peripatetic and physically demanding, Hurlburt's was more settled and orderly. In a letter to Evans, written on December 17, 1838, Hurlburt described his work at Fort William:

"....I commenced school with twelve scholars, but after the return of the fishermen they increased to twenty. Their attendance

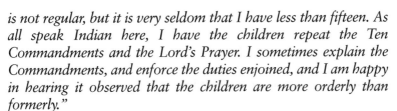

is not regular, but it is very seldom that I have less than fifteen. As all speak Indian here, I have the children repeat the Ten Commandments and the Lord's Prayer. I sometimes explain the Commandments, and enforce the duties enjoined, and I am happy in hearing it observed that the children are more orderly than formerly."

He writes that he has congregations for adult services, *"from thirty to fifty every night"*, and goes on to hope that *"...whether we establish a mission here or not, I hope my residence among them will do them no harm."*

He had two of Evans' syllabary spelling books, he noted, which he used with some of the Indians who attended his school regularly, and was *"...much pleased to see the facility with which the new orthography may be acquired by those uncorrupted with the old."*

"Had I spelling books and hymn-books (in syllabary)," he laments, *"I could easily teach them to read the hymns...I think that a month or six weeks faithful application would enable a person entirely ignorant of letters to read the hymns with fluency. I shall not forget this thought if sent to any new mission in this country. When I take up a translation in another orthography, it makes me sick at heart to see the letters screwed, _contorted and placed in every position to make them say something, and then you can give about as good a guess at the sound as though it were Chinese characters."*

For Evans, things would be very different. Every summer, thousands of Indians from all over the north-west gathered at Saulte St. Marie, where the waters of Lake Superior once crashed through falls and rapids into Lake Huron on their long journey through the Great Lakes into the St. Lawrence, and thence to the Atlantic Ocean. For centuries it had been the location for their summer festivities of hunting, fishing and ritual gatherings, and was a splendid place to meet Indians of all kinds.

Having sent Hurlburt independently to Fort William, Evans left the St. Clair Rapids Mission by canoe for Lake Superior on July 13, 1838. Accompanying him was an Indian missionary of dubious character, Peter Jacobs, who would be his translator. Jacobs' participation had been in some doubt for a while, because he could not leave the settlement until he had discharged his large debts. In a characteristic gesture, Evans paid off all of Jacobs' accounts from the expedition funds in order to allow him to leave. This act would, however, leave Evans himself short of funds for the expedition itself. Meanwhile Mary, Clarissa and Julia Ann were sent to stay with Evans' brother Ephraim, in Cobourg, for the two years he would be away.

If he had been discouraged by the attitude of the British and Foreign Bible Society towards his *Speller* when he left, Evans soon recovered his good humour and his observant and inquisitive nature. In a letter to Mary from Lake Superior, he described what he was finding: *"The pagan Indians are very curious and I play my accordion to attract their attention to my tent in the evening. When they remain for supper, you can imagine what so many mouths do to one flour barrel! We peel off birchbark and make torches by which to fish from the canoe at night to stretch the larder."*

Pushing farther and farther into Indian territory, Evans secured permission from a local Indian chief to establish a mission post on the remote north shore of Lake Superior. Those were hard times indeed. Travelling by canoe, he told Mary, they not infrequently *"...had to knock ice off* (our) *legs and ankles with the handle of a tomahawk."*

But despite letters full of energy and optimism, James Evans was sometimes dismayed at the enormity of the task he had taken on. He wrote to his brother from Lake Superior: *"The poor Indians here are much to be pitied. Their country is the most barren imaginable, nothing but dreary mountains rearing their bare blue summits, and nothing on their sides but a few rabbits..."* The hunting was so poor, he reported, that the mission was constantly being called upon to feed hungry Indians, *"...an old woman living near us last week ate her moccasins and all other leather straps she had..."*

Meanwhile his study of Indian culture continued: *"Mr. Cameron* (the local Hudson's Bay Company Factor) *has a large library at the fort,"* he wrote to Mary, *"which has been made open to me and I am studying the books very hard."*

The Company of Adventurers Trading into Hudson's Bay, later the Hudson's Bay Company, was established by charter in

26

England in 1670 by Charles II. This charter gave the company fur trading privileges over the whole of Manitoba, most of Saskatchewan, the southern half of Alberta, and a large portion of the NorthWest Territories.

Under its charter, the Company had the inalienable power to control trade and administer its huge territory as it saw fit. This is what it did, ruthlessly suppressing any attempts by individuals or competing organizations to engage with it in the fur trade.

At first, the Hudson's Bay Company was in competition with the Companie du Nord, founded in 1676, and with the North-West Fur Trading Company. But the company eventually drove the French out and took over the North-West Fur Trading Company in 1821. This amalgamation increased its influence as far as the Rocky Mountains in the west and to the border with Upper Canada in the east. This now was a monopoly used to subjugate the Indians, tie them and their furs into the Company, and then cheat them on price.

Evans had met George Simpson, the Governor of the Hudson's Bay Company in Canada, on a number of occasions at Fort William, when Simpson was travelling between his lonely company outposts. For him, Fort William was his campaign headquarters away from his main offices at York Factory on Hudson's Bay. Evans began to think about going further north-west to establish missions, a desire which Governor Simpson supported and encouraged. In June 1839, Evans and Peter Jacobs left the Fort William school in the hands of Hurlburt. Together they set out with Indian paddlers and interpreters for Rainy Lake (Lac la Pluie), where upwards of two thousand Indians gathered every summer for medicine feasts. His travels took him through the Red River Settlement (now the site of the city of Winnipeg). There he even found a girl's school, which encouraged him to think of someday bringing Mary and the girls to this remote and exciting outpost in the vast wilderness of the north-west.

However, that would be for a later mission. In the meantime, he returned to Cobourg from his trip to the Lake Superior country early in 1840, to find that the Hudson's Bay Company was encouraging the Wesleyan Methodists to establish missions in its northern territories, an unknown and poorly mapped area of some two million square miles. There was no altruism in the Hudson's Bay Company's motives, needless to say. Their offer was made only to serve their own best interests, for while they were not keen to have 'their' Indians educated and thus capable of questioning the Company and its behaviour, on the other hand, they were aware of the impact that news of the missionaries and their work was having on the Indians of the interior. They, intrigued by the white man's 'speaking bark', were drifting south to the missions at the Red River Settlement and Lake Superior to discover more of these mysteries and leaving their trap lines and hunting areas unattended. This was a situation that the Hudson's Bay Company was not prepared to tolerate. Missions to the northern Indians, under Hudson's Bay Company control and scrutiny, would solve the problem without creating any unnecessary diversions.

Chapter Four

$\mathcal{I}$N THE EARLY SUMMER OF 1840, just a few months after his return from the Lake Superior expedition, Evans set out again. This time he was travelling to establish or direct missions in the north-west at the request of the Hudson's Bay Company. By now Evans and Mary were nearly forty years of age. Clarissa was fourteen and would soon be of marriageable age. Julia Anne Southwind, their adopted Ojibwa daughter who had been Clarissa's companion since childhood, was also at marriageable age. She had returned to her family at the Rice Lake reserve in order to find a suitable husband among her own people.

As a result of the Hudson's Bay Company's invitation to the Methodist Mission Society, four missionaries were sent to the Company's outposts to open missions in the north-west. Evans was appointed General Superintendent of the North-West Indian Missions and went to Norway House. With him went three missionaries: Robert Terrill Rundle, who would eventually move further west to Rocky Mountain House, and ultimately to Fort Edmonton; William Mason who went to Lac la Pluie (Rainy Lake) and Fort Alexander; and George Barnley, sent to be the minister at Moose Factory and Abitibi.

The journey which Evans, Mary and Clarissa made from Cobourg to Norway House in the summer of 1840 was a good eighteen hundred miles. Much of the latter part of it was made by canoe and portage through some of the most majestic but difficult terrain in the world. While they were under way on their two-month voyage, their furniture and other personal property, was shipped from Cobourg back to England, and then out again to York Factory on Hudson's Bay. While longer in distance, this was by far an easier means of transportation than any overland route, with its innumerable portages, would have been. From York Factory, their furniture and personal effects would be shipped in the flat-bottomed York boats down the Nelson River. Even so, the last four hundred miles to Norway House was a journey which included thirty-seven portages, one over a divide more than one thousand feet high.

Evans' original intention, which he had formed at Governor Simpson's request, was for his party to travel with the Governor's party, from Lachine on the St. Lawrence to Fort William on Lake Superior, via lakes Ontario, Erie and Huron, in the big Hudson's Bay Company's 'canots de maître'. From Fort William he expected to travel on to Norway House by the smaller cargo and passenger canoes used in the interior. However, whether as a deliberate snub to distance himself from Evans' mission, or for some unexplained reason of logistics, Simpson left the day before Evans' party arrived at Lachine, taking with him Evans' three fellow missionaries. He left instructions for Evans and his family to travel by steamer to Fort William. They arrived on June 2nd, 1840, after a pleasant trip on the steamship *New England* through the Great Lakes, most of which Mary and Clarissa had never seen before.

Fort William had been built in 1802 by the North-West Trading Co., the Hudson's Bay Company's former early English competitor in the Canadian fur and trapping business, which later folded to become part of the Hudson's Bay Company. With the amalgamation of the two companies, Fort William declined rapidly from its prominent position as a major trading post and cross-roads between the wild north-west and the rest of Upper Canada. As a result of the coming together, the whole of the Hudson's Bay Company's fur business traded out of York Factory, leaving Fort William to become an unimportant staging post and backwater.

Nevertheless, it was still a relatively civilized place to make a stop-over between the known world and the rigours of the wilderness. Here Evans and his family remained for a few days to rest from their journey and to prepare for the much more arduous one to come, which was to be made in a thirty-five foot birchbark canoe. It would have four passengers: Evans, Mary, Clarissa and Peter Jacobs, and nine French 'voyageurs', and would carry almost a ton of freight, such as provisions and bedding. This journey would include dozens of strenuous portages and would take more than a month.

The party began its trek on the Kaministaquia River, with its spectacular portage at Kakabekka Falls, some thirty or so miles north-west of Fort William. Kakabekka, higher than

Niagara Falls, and much more dramatic when the river is in flood, is the 'Great White Falls' of Indian legend.

It was a difficult and energy-sapping trip up-river from Fort William to the Savan Portage on the Dog River. However, after that watershed, the party would enjoy better going since the rivers they were to follow thereafter flowed in the direction of their journey. Even so, there were thirty-five portages from Fort William to Fort Frances, named for Governor Simpson's wife, located on Lac la Pluie.

William Mason was already at Fort Frances when Evans arrived. There the two men had a disagreement. The punctilious Mason did not wish to be left with Peter Jacobs as his interpreter, for he disapproved of the man's reputation and morals. Jacobs had been in trouble several times for both the profligate accumulation of debts and for his relationships with women. Although Evans had counted on the studious, hard-working Henry Steinhauer, another Indian missionary, to accompany him to Norway House, in order to placate Mason, Evans left Steinhauer behind at Fort Frances with Mason, and took the 'difficult' Jacobs on with him to Norway House.

Norway House

Photograph of a sketch of Norway House.

Norway House as it appeared in 1858, from a watercolour by W.H.E. Napier.

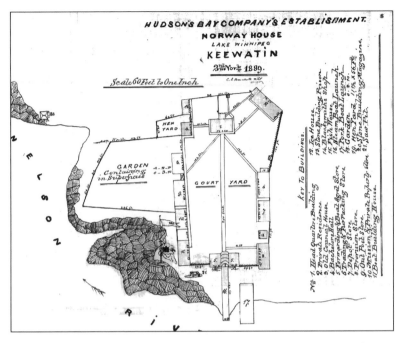

"Hudson's Bay Company's Establishment. Norway House, Lake Winnipeg, Keewatin, November 2, 1889." by C.I. Bouchette.

Norway House, June 1927. Photographer, R. Watson.

Portrait of Sir George Simpson. Black and white engraving by James Scott, 1857 after Stephen Pearce.

Hudson's Bay Company York Boats at Norway House. HBC's 1930 calendar from a painting by Walter J. Phillips.

Early Missionaries.

Cairn dedication at Norway House.

KNOW all Men by these Presents, That I, *George Marsden*
President of the **Wesleyan Methodist Church** in British North America,
under the protection of ALMIGHTY GOD, and with an eye single to His glory, by the
imposition of my hands and prayer, (being assisted by the Ministers present,) have this
day set apart *James Evans* for the office of a **Minister**
in the said Church; a man who, in the judgment of the CONFERENCE, is well qualified
for that work: and he is hereby recommended to all whom it may concern, as a
proper person to administer the Sacraments and Ordinances, and to feed the flock of
CHRIST, so long as his spirit and practice are such as become the Gospel of CHRIST.

IN TESTIMONY WHEREOF, I have hereunto set my hand and seal. this
Sixth day of *October* in the year of our Lord, one thousand
eight hundred and thirty *three*

York, Upper Canada

George Marsden

*Certificate of Evans' ordination as a Minister in
the Wesleyan Methodist Church in British
North America.*

STATUTORY DECLARATION

DOMINION OF CANADA, |
Province **ғоииту** оf ...ALBERTA......... }
To Wit: |

In the~~xxxxxxx~~ of The Matter of The Translation
of the English language into the Cree language
and the invention of the Cree syllabics.

I, Robert B. Steinhauer, Resident Missionary

of the United Church of Canada, Saddle Lake, ... in the

Province
County of .... Alberta.

Do solemnly declare that

(1) To the best of my knowledge and belief, my late father, the
Reverend Henry B. Steinhauer with the assistance of the late
John Sinclair, layman, translated the English Bible into the
Cree language.

(2) That this is borne out by records- for reference of which I quote
the following as being a true excerpt of Reverend J. E. Sanderson's
book on "Messengers of the Churches" (second series) Page 139, which
reads as follows:-
"While James Evans was inventing the syllabic characters, Henry
Steinhauer with the assistance of John Sinclair, was translating the
Scriptures into the Cree language. The manuscripts when completed,
were entrusted to the Rev., W. Mason, then going to England, to be
printed by the Bible Society. Mr. Mason who subsequently left the
Methodist Church for the Church of England, had his own name
inserted as the translator and even claimd celebrity as to the
invention of the syllabic characters."

(3) That to the best of my knowledge and belief, my late father, Rev.,
Henry B. Steinhauer with the assistance of the late John Sinclair,
were directly instrumental in the translation of the Scriptures
into the Cree language and that I have no record and do not know
of any record of Rev., W. Mason or any other person having taking
any part in the work of translating the Scriptures as undertaken
by my late father with the assistance of the late John Sinclair.

And I make this Solemn Declaration conscientiously believing it to be true, and knowing that it is of the
same force and effect as if made under oath, and by virtue of "The Canada Evidence Act."

DECLARED BEFORE ME AT.......Saddle Lake

Province
in the County of.................Alberta

this..21st..day of ....May.................1936.

FORM NO. 130

.... q
Indian Agent.

*William Mason's claim to have done a major part of the translation
of the Scriptures, and even his claim to have invented the syllabic
alphabet, were formally refuted in this declaration by Robert
Steinhauer, son of Evans' friend and collaborator, Henry Steinhauer.*

37

Chapter Five

*T*HE NELSON RIVER starts its journey to the Arctic Ocean at the north-eastern tip of Lake Winnipeg, flows through a number of lakes, and eventually empties into Hudson's Bay.

Around the year 1819, two Norwegian carpenters built a fort for the Hudson's Bay Company on a rocky promontory some miles north of the point where the Nelson River begins its independent life. It took the name Norway House from its builders.

Evans and his party arrived at Norway House at dawn on July 26, 1840. They camped overnight at Playgreen Point and then made their way to Norway House on Playgreen Lake. It seems that this area was so named because it was the place where the first white people to explore the area had seen Indians playing a ball game with an inflated animal's bladder.

Norway House was Governor Simpson's headquarters when he was touring his north-western territories. It was a busy and extensive place, protected behind a twenty foot high palisade, of the type common to most of the Company's posts. In addition to the governor's quarters, other buildings included a long mess hall where visiting officers of the Company met for council meetings, and cottages for the many apprentices. These were the people who learned the rudiments of the Company's business at Norway House before being sent to one or other of its outposts west of the Rockies, up in the Arctic Circle, in distant Oregon, or to other equally remote postings. There was a counting house with the high stools of the period, along with desks and ledgers. To support the huge trade both into and out of the interior, there were warehouses, storerooms and fur packing sheds, as well as trade shops for the carpenter, boat-builders, blacksmith and other necessary artisans.

In 1970, in her book, *Reservations are for Indians*, Heather Robinson wrote a bleak description of Norway House's situation:

"The lake (Winnipeg) *is messy about dying. Much of it just oozes away for miles on either side of the Nelson's banks, forming great stretches of muskeg covered with straggly spruce, scrub and coarse grass. A few rocky promontories jut*

out from the squishy morass. A man can sink up to his waist or, in fact, out of sight in this bog when it is wet in the spring. It can grow grass but it is almost always too wet to allow cattle to eat it or men to mow it. In the summer, the muskeg produces clouds of mosquitoes which rise like a pestilence from stagnant pools...

"...Norway House is a dank and dark place. The air is heavy and damp even in winter. The lowness, flatness of Norway House are sensible, tangible, immediately—a shallow bowl with slippery sides..."

"...The river itself is huge and sprawling, dwarfing the dull, monotonous trees. Near Rossville, two miles across, it is almost a lake. It flows everywhere, forming channels, streams, bays and inlets.... The river reduces the human to insignificance..."

From the beginning, Norway House had a perpetual air of movement and transience, for it stood at the confluence of all of the major water routes flowing from the prairies and the north-west to Hudson's Bay. Europeans who had landed from Europe on ships docking at York Factory, passed through on their way south to the Red River Settlements and the prairies. Explorers and traders used Norway House as a staging post on their journeys westward, and furs were shipped northwards through the fort to York Factory, on their way to Europe.

As he familiarized himself with his new posting, Evans would find boats of all shapes and sizes the recurring reality of Norway House. Boats from the Red River district, the dashing and boisterous Saskatchewan river crews and the fantastically-painted Indian canoes from around Fort William, all tied up at Norway House's docks. Above all he was to learn to recognize, and then admire, the famous Portage la Loche brigade. This seasoned crew would make a journey of upwards of sixth months from the Red River to Hudson's Bay and back, carrying furs out of the interior, and gathering even greater cargoes of furs from trappers and other boat crews along the way. They would take all the furs to York Factory and then bring the necessities of life and trade back from the British ships to the trading posts and settlements of Manitoba and Saskatchewan. When he first saw the York boats of the la Loche boys, Evans could not have known how integral a part of his life they were

to become, nor how they would come to regard him as one of their own.

Much to the chagrin of the managers of the other Hudson's Bay Company forts and trading establishments of the interior, Governor Simpson, an autocratic and didactic little man whom the Factors called 'Little Napoleon', usually chose Norway House as the site of the annual council of the Hudson's Bay Company. At the council, Simpson would meet with his Factors and chief traders from all over the interior and the north-west to discuss company business, make promotions, assign territories and mete out discipline as was necessary. At such meetings, the Governor would lay down the law about how the Company's men should deport themselves, including whether they would have his permission to marry, take a vacation away from their post, or bring their children out from England or Scotland. He lived a strict and economical life himself and expected frugality of his people. He insisted that so far as was possible, they should live off the land and not charge the company with unnecessary expenses. In particular he insisted that they should refrain from seeking to import frivolous goods from Great Britain, because such articles took up space which could more profitably be allocated for money-earning cargo. Many were the Factors or managers who smarted from a public reprimand at a council meeting for ordering from London such items as mustard, impractical articles of clothing, or baubles of haberdashery for their wives or sweethearts.

For more than seven years, Simpson's secretary at the annual meeting had been Donald Ross, the Chief Factor at Norway House. It was Ross's responsibility to ensure that the Governor achieved his full agenda at the annual meeting. It was Ross who was left behind to smooth ruffled feathers when Simpson had passed on his way once more. Ross and Evans were to become close friends and allies for a time, although in the end, the demands on Ross' loyalty to the Company eventually led to a hurtful rupture in their relationship. But that was to come later. As Evans gazed upon the place which was to be his new home, and met his new neighbours, he must have enjoyed strong sensations of expectation and pleasure at the thought of what the next years were to bring in the way of challenges, novelties and successes.

At this point, it may be appropriate to consider the condition of the Indians of the interior. When the first white people, explorers, trappers and traders, began to infiltrate Indian lands in the interior, the Indians outnumbered the whites by ten to one, until they were decimated by smallpox between 1818 and 1821.

The predominating peoples of the land between Hudson's Bay and Lake Superior were the Cree. Estimates put their numbers at around fifteen thousand in the early 17th century, when white adventurers and hunters first began to encounter them. However, since families and clans elided unnoticeably into each other, it is difficult to say with any certainty who, or how many, they were.

Cree, the name the white people came to call them, is derived from 'Kristenaux'. This label was the French corruption of the Indians' own name for themselves, although they also called themselves the Nehiyowuk, or 'exact people'. Closely related to the Ojibwa, their social organization was very similar, as was the physical reality of their lives, their homes, their religion and observations, and even their way of hunting and fishing. They wore clothes of painted and fringed moose-skin leather, fringed leather leggings, breechcloths, and caps of beaver and caribou skins. In their homes they slept under blankets of rabbit skin or cleaned and softened furs. Their vessels were made of wood, birchbark, and soapstone. In any Cree community, it was the women who did the bulk of the work. Among their many and varied tasks, was the preparation of huge quantities of pemmican. This food of dried pulverized meat, mixed with caribou fat, was their staple both through the winter and for the extremely long journeys they frequently made to their hunting grounds on foot, or by canoe, snowshoe or sled.

The influx of Europeans, with their cornucopia of trade goods to pay for the furs brought to them by the Indians, meant that in a short time few Indians lived much further than fifteen miles from a trading post. They trapped intensively and sold their pelts to the white traders at the Hudson's Bay Company forts, taking trade goods such as weapons, knives, blankets and frequently alcohol in payment. Furthermore, by supplying them with guns and ammunition, the Europeans ensured that there would be struggles for turf between the Indians which would prevent them from organizing and co-operating in their own shared interests. The Cree and the Assiniboine moved west and south in search of game and furs, bringing about an inevitable conflict with the Prairie Indians such as the Blackfoot and Mandans. The Ojibwa moved north and west into the vacuum created by the movement of the Cree. But for all of them, the new reality was one of severely depleted game and fur stocks. Indeed, by 1840, beaver, moose, caribou and even the humble rabbit had been hunted or trapped almost to the point of extinction. The ecology of Indian life and tradition was severely compromised, forcing the Indians' into an even greater reliance on the white people for their welfare.

The depredations of alcohol, the clash of cultures and recurring epidemics of smallpox in the 1830s led to the further degradation of Indian life and society. Within thirty more years, the Indians of the interior were hangers-on at the edge of the white man's commercial feast. Despair, unrest, humiliation and their ultimate dispersal to reservations followed.

But this, too, was all to come. When the Evans' family arrived at Norway House, they found a trading post which had been established in 1819 by the Hudson's Bay Company four hundred miles north of Winnipeg, on the natural water-highway between Winnipeg and the Hudson's Bay. Boats headed for the Athabasca and Mackenzie Rivers also passed by Norway House, the last settled European presence they would encounter for many hundreds of miles.

Stepping ashore, Evans' party was to discover that Governor Simpson had already left without waiting to meet the new Superintendent of Missions, a characteristic and calculated slight of the kind he frequently meted out to those who had different expectations of him. Instead, Evans and his family were met by Donald Ross, his wife and family, and by the young English missionary, Robert Rundle, who was soon to be despatched to the new mission at Fort Edmonton on the Prairies.

Ross was Scottish, a big, heavy-set man with an equally large wife and six children. He had the capacity to encourage the best in those whose lives he governed because he was strict, fair and generous. He showed James and Mary to their new

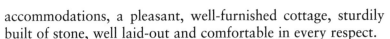

accommodations, a pleasant, well-furnished cottage, sturdily built of stone, well laid-out and comfortable in every respect.

For his part, the keen and capable young Rundle had already begun to establish the work of the mission at Norway House. He had started to teach the Indian children, had conducted baptisms, weddings and burials, and had kept a register of attendees at his Sunday services. Awaiting Evans' arrival, he had engaged a Swampy Cree, Thomas Hassell, as the mission's interpreter, and recommended Evans to keep him on at Norway House as a teacher in due course. Hassell had been educated in the mission school at the Red River Settlement and was a thoroughly likeable, honest and hard-working young man. He spoke English, French, Cree and Chipeweyan, the difficult language spoken by Indians who lived at the most north-westerly limit of the territory Evans intended to cover. Hassell had been at school in Red River for eight years, under the tutelage of his guardian there, the Rev. David Jones, a missionary from England. He then had entered service with the Hudson's Bay Company, but at Evans' request, Ross released him to become his personal interpreter and guide, and ultimately a teacher at the school yet to be set up.

Evans and Hassell immediately liked each other, as did Evans and Ross. Ross liked Evans because the latter lacked the usual pomposity of the missionaries he had met. As well, Evans was thoroughly grounded in Indian lore and culture from his years of working with the Ojibwa in Upper Canada and around Lake Superior. It was an added advantage, in Ross' eyes, that Evans seemed quite familiar with the Hudson's Bay Company's culture, so he anticipated that Evans would not give him the problems that some of the more arrogant and ignorant missionaries gave at other Company posts. For his part, Evans liked the Factor for his blunt honesty, good humour, kindness and willingness to co-operate.

However, times were changing. By the time the Methodists were negotiating with the Hudson's Bay Company for permission to open missions in the north-west, based on the Company's series of fortified trading posts, there were already deep-rooted and ultimately cataclysmic changes beginning to happen in the Company's sphere of influence.

Tired of being treated in the habitually cavalier manner of the Hudson's Bay Company, which set whatever rates it wanted for the furs they brought in, more and more Indians were bypassing the Company. They were leaving their traplines to head south, especially towards the newly-opening Red River country. There, independent traders, and particularly entrepreneurial Americans, were offering better prices, better trade goods, and alcohol. Two tin cups of liquor were worth a buffalo robe; four gallons a good horse. Many were the Indians who lost a winter's hard work to the ravages of the traders' specially set-up drinking dens, such as the notorious Fort Whoop-up.

To counter these development, it was Ross who had originally suggested to Simpson that the Methodists be permitted to set up a mission at Norway House. This move, it was hoped, would help keep Indian trappers from migrating to the Red River area.

For their part, the officers of the Hudson's Bay Company realized that missionaries, by the nature of their work, were agents of change whereas the company's continued profitability and success depended on the Indians continuing to pursue their traditional ways and skills. The position of being caught between the rock of unfolding events and the hard place of the missionary's role in the inevitability of change, may explain why the Hudson's Bay Company and Evans fell out. As Donald Ross pointed out, settled Indians did not produce equal returns.

To counteract the mission as an agent of unwelcome change, by 1825 the Hudson's Bay Company had drawn up a policy for coping with the unsettling influence of the missionaries at its trading posts. These missionaries were not to impose their moral scruples on Company officials and their way of doing business. They were to build their missions only at company posts. They were to teach company servants, minister to them, and develop their mission only with those Indians who deliberately sought knowledge of the basics of Christianity and English language. They should promote agriculture in poor areas, but not at the expense of the Indians' commitment to hunt and trap for the Company. They were not to spend much time in Indian encampments, where they could disturb the Indians' traditional way of life. They could not establish a mission where it would be financially burdensome to the Company. Above all else, they were not to meddle with the Company in its trading processes. This was the unwritten, but surely acknowledged, basis of Evans' establishing the mission at Rossville. Indeed, he must have agreed with Simpson that if he were allowed to establish a mission, he would not try to influence the Indians against the Company in any way. This should be born in mind in the light of the accusation, later, that it was the Company which reneged on its obligation to Evans and the Methodists. On the contrary, it seems to have been the other way around.

Chapter Six

*A*T A BRIEF MEETING IN EARLY AUGUST, shortly after Evans' party had arrived at Norway House, Ross invited him to take a journey with him to the Hudson's Bay Company headquarters at York Factory on Hudson's Bay. Ross was going there to procure supplies and meet his oldest daughter on her return from school in London. Evans knew that there was mission business to be done at York Factory, including picking up the books, paper and other equipment that he and his other three colleagues would need at their widely-flung mission stations. Here was an opportunity. He was glad to begin the work of discovering the people and the country which were to be his 'parish'. In his absence, the indefatigable Rundle would secure the help of local Indians to build a school and a church on Playgreen Island, a mile or two distant in the lake from Norway House. Already, Evans was keen to move there, to establish his mission at a good remove from the boisterous temptations and the comings and goings of the fort.

The journey to York Factory was made in seven heavily-laden York boats, carrying between them the season's furs, which would be packed and sent to England. It was critically important to catch the returning ships before the ice set in and prevented them from departing. The crew of their canoes were men of the famous Portage la Loche brigade, who regularly stopped at Norway House on their way north from Winnipeg to York Factory. Along with Evans was Hassell his guide and interpreter, who was soon to be his friend as well.

The Portage La Loche brigade was composed of two dozen paddlers, hand-picked by the Governor himself from among the best in the north-west. The crew took its name from the daunting task of making the notorious twelve mile portage at la Loche. This watershed, where the rivers divided, draining eastward into Hudson Bay, or north and west into the Arctic and the Pacific Oceans, was a dreaded climb of eight hundred feet in twelve miles.

Reaching Portage la Loche, the men emptied the boats of their cargo of supplies for other Company outposts, and carried the load in ninety pound packs to the summit. There they met other crews from northern and western outposts who were bringing their furs in to be loaded onto the York Factory boats. At the summit the two groups traded their cargoes, the la Loche brigade leaving the trade goods and supplies for their northern and western comrades to portage back to their own boats. They then descended the twelve-mile portage back to the York boats, each carrying two ninety pound packages of furs on the grueling downhill leg, to resume their journey to York Factory. The la Loche brigade regularly made the journey between the Red River Settlements and York Factory, a six-month trip which began in May each year, arriving at York Factory with a cargo worth as much as $40,000.

Thus, there was a constant shuttling to and fro, with furs going to York Factory, and food, trade goods and other materials being shipped out of York Factory for the Hudson's Bay Company posts in the interior. The Portage la Loche brigade took furs north and brought supplies south to Norway House, where other crews from all over the interior picked up what they needed and ferried the goods to their own home posts and settlements. Boats from Fort Edmonton, the Mackenzie River settlements, the Red River settlements and the Saskatchewan River country, all met at Norway House to bring furs for collection and take on cargo for the return journey.

The York boat crews earned every penny of their wages with hard back-breaking labour. When conditions prevented the boats from sailing under their big, white sails, the boatmen were reduced to poling or rowing them through shallow water, or through the narrow, rushing water of the innumerable rapids they encountered. And frequently, sometimes several times a day, they arrived at portages, where everything in the boats had to be unloaded and carried to the next leg of their passage. Incidental tasks included hunting, cooking, making camp and often surveying the land. For this daily round of labour, the regular oarsmen, the 'middlemen', earned £17 per year, the steersman £21 and the bosun £20. The Company provided them with their basic requirements of food, tea and pemmican, but they took everything else they needed from the bounty of the land through which they travelled. Fish, game, deer and anything else they could catch with their lines and nets, or bring down with their guns, provided their sustenance.

Evans reached York Factory with Ross and the la Loche brigade on August 12. There he found a busy, but dull, settlement which had been founded as Fort Nelson, on the banks of the Nelson River in 1682, the oldest settlement in the north. The landscape around York Factory was bare of trees and interminably flat. This was the centre that the Hudson's Bay Company's boats came to from England during the brief season when the Bay was free of ice, bringing goods for the Company's many trading posts and forts, and returning to London with precious cargoes of furs. When a ship came in, the company men worked from four a.m. to midnight or later, dealing with its cargo, logging what was unloaded, and re-assigning goods to whatever location they were directed.

As he acquainted himself with the settlement, Evans would first have observed that it was full of labourers, unloading and loading the boats which had made it to the port through the short summer. All were in a hurry to leave to avoid being locked in the ice for the winter. But then, as he began to take in the details of the place, he would have noted that York Factory was, indeed, the most substantial settlement he had been in since he had left Fort William on his way to Norway House. It was comprised of good houses for the chief trader and his assistants, a guest house, and barracks for the unmarried men. As well, there was a storeroom for whale oil, which was reduced to make lamp oil, and also used for waterproofing the coarse cloth used to cover the exposed cargoes in the York boats and big cargo canoes. Included were a tin shop, a forge, a carpenter's shop and facilities for all the other trades and services such an enterprise needed. A largely-permanent complement of three dozen white men ran the fort. Only two women were in permanent residence; the wife of George Gladman, the company accountant, and Letitia Hargrave, wife of the manager, James Hargrave, who was herself newly-arrived from England.

Evans and Hargrave quickly found mutual interests and established a mutual regard. Though he was a younger man, among the Hudson's Bay Company men at York Factory and in the north-west, Hargrave was the most like Evans in his simple,

robust faith and his ability to deal with details while keeping the larger picture clear and focused. He had been passed over for promotion by the mercurial Governor Simpson on at least two occasions, but still managed York Factory, the most difficult posting in the company, with skill, energy and honesty.

During his days there, Evans busied himself with missionary work among the local Indian and Inuit people at the fort. There was much regular employment for his skill in first aid and medicine, as well as his missionary's talents in preaching and leading the singing of hymns and psalms. For his part, Ross reacquainted himself with his daughter, who had returned from England on one of the ships. All who had come from Norway House, or from even further in the interior, enjoyed the increased buzz of activity and the opportunity for wider socializing.

But after a few days, the York boats pushed out into the river to begin their return to Norway House, only this time they were moving against the current. It was grueling work for the boatmen, much of it either poling through fast-running shallows and rapids, or dragging the boat from the shore with tumplines and harnesses. Evans' willingness to help in these situations, and his general sympathy for the lonely, dangerous durance of the men's lives, endeared him to them. Again his attitude set him aside from the general run of the officers and other 'bourgeois', who chose to have very little human contact with them. It was this empathy with the boatmen which led to Evans' eventual rupture with Simpson, Ross and the Hudson's Bay Company. It was Evans who took the crew's side in demanding a day of rest on the Sabbath, while Simpson was adamant they should continue to work every day of the short trans-shipping season.

On his return to Norway House, Evans found that Rundle and his helpers had constructed a school already, and had gathered the timber necessary to build the church, on which they hoped to begin immediately. Nevertheless, Evans and his family continued to live at their comfortable stone house at Norway House as they waited for the structure to be ready and the mission house to accommodate them. Evans canoed over to the school and back every day to tend to his growing band of followers. Already word of his work there had spread beyond the immediate area around Norway House. Indians had begun arriving from all points of the compass to take advantage of the school and the other facilities he was developing for them. In all of this Ross, 'Big Donald' as he was known, was Evans' constant support and encouragement. To show his appreciation, Evans named the mission Rossville, although his wife Mary had hoped it would be called Evansville instead.

With winter, the best and easiest time to travel, setting in, Rundle left for the newly established mission at Fort Edmonton on September 7, 1840. At the same time, Clarissa left to go to school at the Red River Settlement. These must have been somber times in the Evans household, for Evans had become fond of his capable, modest young daughter while Mary would have felt the loss of her company keenly.

Chapter Seven

*A*T ROSSVILLE, Evans began instructing the children of the local Indians. He taught them English, some mathematics, writing and religion, although he knew the HBC would quickly see that even such a basic education would make it more difficult for the company to keep the Indians ignorant and compliant. Undoubtedly, it was at this time that the seeds were sown of Evans' subsequent rupture with the Hudson's Bay Company and with its loyal servant, Donald Ross.

Evans knew that for the Indians to profit from an education, they would have to be able to read and write in their own language. He knew, also, that he was the only one who would provide them with the tools to do so. He quickly observed that the language of the Cree was built principally of thirty-six sounds alone, often linked together into long, long words. This was not unlike the way some German nouns are built from their component ideas, in which one word could do the business of a complete sentence in English. In addition, Evans recognized that Cree and Ojibwa, for which he had already developed an alphabet during his work with the latter in Upper Canada, were basically similar. It seemed reasonable to believe that he could produce an alphabet for the Cree language not very different from the one he had already developed for the Ojibwa. Presumably some relatively minor refinements and modifications would accommodate the differences between the two languages. With his previous experience to guide him, and remembering his youthful training in shorthand as a young merchant's clerk in London, Evans realized that a sequence of patterns, not unlike shorthand, could be modified to do duty in representing the sounds of Cree. This realization was the foundation of Evans' Cree syllabic alphabet, a development which would profoundly change the life and outlook of the Cree Indians of Rossville, and those far beyond.

Evans worked on his syllabics alone. When he had a system he thought would work, he tried it out with Mary before introducing it to his Indian charges. The two Indian teachers, Thomas Hassell and Peter Jacobs, and some of the older and more clever children picked it up in less than a day. Even the less experienced children could learn to read simple texts without much effort. The news spread quickly. At dinner with Ross one evening, Evans showed his syllabics to the Factor and some visiting company officers from Oxford House, a company post midway between Norway House and York Factory. By the end of the evening, everyone gathered at Ross's house knew that what Evans had developed would have universal ramifications. This could be not only an alphabet for the Cree, but also for the Plains Indians on the Prairies, and for those as far away as the Inuit in the Arctic Circle.

Of his work at that time, Evans wrote in a letter of September 15: "*I commenced a school on the opposite side of the river* (from Norway House) *and had about 25 scholars anxious to learn, teaching them to read the English and their own tongue.*"

On December 3, he observed that, "*The short time which is required to learn to read and write arises from there being no such thing as learning to spell, every character in the alphabet being a syllable, so that when these are learned, all is learned.*"

By the following summer, in a June 1841 letter, he would be able to record that, "*The men, women and children of Norway House write and read it* (syllabics) *with ease and fluency, as do some European gentlemen who speak the language of the Indians.*"

With the evidence of the success of his alphabet, Evans was encouraged to imagine how he might build upon his achievements. In a letter of October 19, he indicated the way his mind was turning: "*Several of the boys are beginning to read the written hymns in the Cree character,*" he wrote, "*and I yet feel encouraged to think I can print them in a few days.*"

Clearly, to propagate the gospel more effectively and to reach a wider audience, Evans realized he needed to have printed material in sufficient quantity. Such requisite quantity could not be supplied by the painstaking labour of himself, Mary and his Indian assistants, writing texts by hand.

In one of her many witty and perceptive letters, Letitia Hargrave refers to Evans' desire for a printing press at

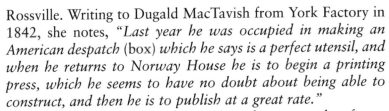

Rossville. Writing to Dugald MacTavish from York Factory in 1842, she notes, *"Last year he was occupied in making an American despatch* (box) *which he says is a perfect utensil, and when he returns to Norway House he is to begin a printing press, which he seems to have no doubt about being able to construct, and then he is to publish at a great rate."*

But developing a way of printing took two months of continuous labour, as Evans experimented with different methods to achieve the results he wanted. On September 28 he wrote: *"For a fortnight I have been endeavouring to cast type to print the Cree language, but every attempt hitherto has failed. I have no proper materials, neither type metal, nor any other thing requisite. I hope, however...to begin printing the Cree language in a few weeks or months at furthest."*

Two days later, he noted that he had *"...cut types in lead of two characters and took moulds in clay, chalk, putty and sand, and tried some other fruitless experiments."* And on October 13, he described a new attempt in which he had *"...cast a plate of hardened lead, polished it and commenced cutting the Cree alphabet, making a sort of stereotyped plate."* He finished making the plate two nights later, on October 15, recording in his diary: *"Last night I finished the alphabet plate, and today I printed a few sheets."*

But a stereotype plate, while an improvement on handwritten texts, was still not satisfactory. It still required the labour of writing out the text on the plate and then printing from it. Evans needed movable type of the kind used throughout Europe to produce books. He found a solution in very simple process. Cutting a mould by hand, with the character reversed, he filled it with molten lead which he had obtained by stripping the thin lead linings from a Hudson's Bay Company tea-chest. One by one, he cut the characters of the syllabic alphabet and moulded them, making a sufficient quantity of each character before moving on to the next one he needed. It was a slow and painstaking business, but it provided him with founts of type which could be used over and over again. For paper, which was in short supply at the mission, Evans stripped and used the white inner surfaces of the silver birch. Ingeniously he adapted a fur-packing press to provide himself with a printing press. In just such an inventive, temporizing way was the *Rossville Mission Press* established, the first printing operation to be established outside the regular centres of population in Upper and Lower Canada.

At first, Evans did all of the printing work himself, but he still had his responsibilities as Superintendent of the north-west to fulfill. Often he was away for very long periods of time. To maintain the printing work in his absence, he trained a number of Indians to help him, and in due course they took the work over, while he continued to travel, teach and preach.

Of his invention, Lord Dufferin, the Governor General of Canada, said on one occasion to the great Canadian Methodist, Dr. Egerton Ryerson Young: "*Why Mr. Young, what a blessing to humanity is the man who invented that alphabet. ... The fact is, the nation has given many a man a title, and a pension, and then a resting-place and a monument in Westminster Abbey, who never did half so much for his fellow creatures.*"

Indians for hundreds of miles around, hearing about this new development, were keen to learn. Being adept students, they didn't wait for a white man to teach them, but taught each other. In a letter of 1855, Thomas Hurlburt, who became Superintendent at Norway House after Evans' death, noted that two of his missionaries were sent out from Norway House to the Chippeweyans on the northern borders of the Cree country. There they were surprised to discover that the Chippewayans were already able to read well in Cree, although they had never had a mission or a missionary in their midst. Rather, they learned from borrowed or stolen Cree books, learning in the Cree language rather than modifying it to accommodate the differences between it and their own because, as Hurlburt noted, "*...all who wished to be thought genteel and well bred must speak Cree.*"

In time, Evans' syllabics were adopted by all the Christian denominations doing missionary work among the Indians. Eventually his system was adapted to suit the needs of many other tribes. Archdeacon MacDonald, an Anglican missionary, modified it for the Tukudh, the Reverend Fr. Morrice adapted it for the Indians at his mission at Stuart Lake, and the Reverend

John MacLean taught it to the Blackfoot on the prairies. By 1853, seven years after Evans' death, the mission at Oxford House, and many other missions in the north and north-west, had their own presses. By 1860 most of the Christian missions were using Evans' syllabary alphabet either wholly or in substantial part. Thus, in twenty years, books printed in Evans' syllabics had become the vehicle of choice for both Indians and missionaries in the Algonkian setting. The first complete version of the Bible printed in an Indian language was printed in Swampy Cree in 1861. The Plains Cree had theirs by 1920.

Shortly after producing his first printed book, this the first book printed in the Canadian north, no less, and presenting the first copy off the press to Mary, Evans left by canoe for a tour of the Indian villages around the shores of Lake Winnipeg. He took family letters to Cobourg and England with him. But most importantly, he carried copies of his printed book to be sent to the British and Foreign Missionary Society in London. In a letter to his brother Ephraim, attending a church conference in England, Evans urged him to do everything in his power to get the Society to accept his syllabics and to print missionary material in them.

I have written to the Hudson's Bay Company Commission headquarters in London asking for permission to import a small printing press, fully aware of their policy to allow no such device into their territory. They doubtless fear that the spread of knowledge will endanger their hold on the hunters. But I beg you to use all your persuasive powers to make the Company Committee see the evil there is in keeping these people in ignorance. The fur traders cannot hope to monopolize this great land forever; they must give way to immigration. What then of the Indian? The people must be prepared to meet settlement.

It was an extraordinarily perceptive and enlightened letter.

In a letter to Dugald MacTavish from York Factory in September 1842, the equally perceptive, but more waspishly tempered Letitia Hargrave expressed the commonly held view of the Hudson's Bay Company's attitude towards the Indians. The Jesuits had set up a college among the Indians and Mrs. Hargrave writes of the Company giving one hundred pounds to a Mr. Blanchette to be Principal of the college, *"...whether as a retaining fee, that he may keep the Indians as we wish them to be, or because they wish well to him and his labors, I can't say, but I think the former."*

Giving a glimpse of the tensions between the different Christian groups vying to save the souls of the Indians, she reports that, *"Mr. Blanchette is an excellent old man who appears to mind his own affairs, while the Episcopal missionaries here attend only to other peoples."* She mentions the habit of missionaries from one church who *"...go about rechristening Indians and children who have been baptized by Mr. Evans, while the Wesleyans revile the Roman Catholic clergy of the Settlement."* Evans, she goes on, *"...says his instructions are to go only where there is no minister of another sect, but the others hate him with all their heart."*

All previous accounts of Evans' life and work have promoted the notion that Evans spoke Ojibwa and Cree fluently and was the sole 'inventor' of the system used to write their language. However, a number of sources in the Indian community, including Stan McKay, the Director of a centre for Indian studies in Winnipeg, contend that Evans spoke only a little Cree. He, therefore, could not have done the translations he is credited with because of his lack of knowledge of the language. Furthermore, it is probable that the Methodist mission at Rossville was not as successful as the Roman Catholic mission at Norway House because Evans did not speak Cree, while the Roman Catholic missionaries did. McKay claims that the received wisdom concerning Evans and the Cree syllabics has also tended to overshadow the contribution to the translation work done by three of the other Methodist missionaries, William Mason, Henry Steinhauer and Benjamin Sinclair. Both Sinclair, being Cree from Norway House, and Steinhauer, the Indian missionary who often had accompanied Evans, would have had a greater familiarity with structure of the language.

However, writing about the matter in *The Gift to a Nation of a Written Language* in 1911, the Rev. Nathaniel Burwash quotes a letter written by Mason which clearly states that Evans was the inventor of the syllabary alphabet.

"I never claimed to be the inventor of the Cree syllabary,"

56

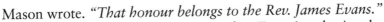

Mason wrote. *"That honour belongs to the Rev. James Evans."*

There is other evidence, too, for Evans' role in the development of the syllabics. In an excerpt from his book, *Hudson's Bay*, R.M. Ballantyne writes, *"In fine weather I used to visit my friend, Mr. Evans, at Rossville, when I always had a warm welcome... I spent a pleasant afternoon in sauntering about the village and in admiring the rapidity and ease with which the Indians could read and write the Indian language by means of a syllabic alphabet invented by their clergyman."*

Among the Algonkian peoples, the Cree were known as 'the exact people', and their language was always regarded as the classic form of the Algonkian languages, much as the Edinburgh Scots believe they speak English in its purest and most agreeable form. It is difficult now to ascertain with any degree of confidence exactly who was responsible for what. But together, it is clear, the missionaries and the Indians found that they could relatively easily adapt Evans' work with the language of the Ojibwa Indians and modify it to the demands of the different form of Cree.

As Superintendent of all of the north-western missions, Evans had the responsibility of visiting and overseeing the work of the other Methodist missions spread out over an unimaginably vast area of the Canadian north-west. Travelling was easier in the winter. On December 14, 1840, Evans set off on a three month tour of Indian camps and company posts spread out over a six-hundred mile area that included the lakes Winnipeg, Manitoba, Winnipegosis and a dozen others. He was accompanied by Hassell and two other young Indian men who hoped to learn much from their association with the good-natured, fearless and hard-working missionary who led their party.

It was a hard trip for the sled-dogs as much as for the humans. In his diary, Evans noted that they had to carry *"...about forty small flannel bags in which* (the dogs') *feet are thrust"* when their feet became cut and sore from the roughness of the ice over which they often travelled. And everywhere he went, Evans found that his reputation for giving the Indians a written language had preceded him. Everywhere he was met with great affection and acclaim. For his own part, wherever he went among the Indians of the Interlake country, he baptized children,

taught, conducted services and exercised his medical skills.

In letters full of news and endearments, James wrote to Mary frequently during his absence. These letters would change hands as many as six or seven times as they made their way from wherever he was, at established settlements such as Grand Rapids or Le Pas, or at nameless Indian encampments in the wilderness, to Mary at Rossville. In his absence she was filling her husband's place in many ways, encouraging and supporting the Indians whose lives were harder in every respect than the lives of the Indians Mary and James had known at Rice Lake or at other missions in which they had served in Upper Canada.

Evans returned to Rossville in March 1841 to find that good news had come from England. The Missionary Society had agreed to send him the press he had requested through the good offices of his brother, Ephraim. The announcement carried the rider that the Hudson's Bay Company had insisted that the new press should be used only to print missionary material and that, in any case, everything had to be submitted to Donald Ross for his approval, on behalf of the Company, before it could be distributed among the Indians. Evans was annoyed by the pettiness of the restriction, but the victory of being allowed a press at all outweighed his disappointment. It is likely that he may have reasoned with himself that Big Donald was a decent, God-fearing and amenable fellow, who would not put unnecessary hindrances in his way.

With great plans for the work he would do when a proper printing press arrived, he returned with a will to his cobbled-together printing office. There he set about preparing and printing religious tracts, hymn sheets and bible readings for his school and for distribution to the Indians of Rossville and the territories beyond. Increasingly, large numbers of Indians were coming to Rossville in search of books and material to read in their own language. It was an extraordinary achievement which, Evans could see, would make massive changes to the Indians and their way of life. This experience, he believed, would help prepare them for the day when they would have to meet invading hordes of immigrants arriving in their formerly-unknown lands, and they, the Indians, would have to deal with them.

In 1842 Evans had the *Rossville Mission Press* working at

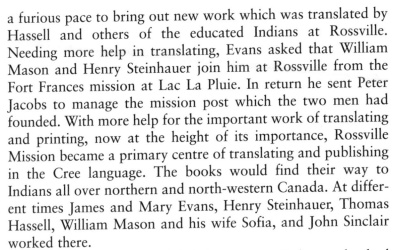

a furious pace to bring out new work which was translated by
Hassell and others of the educated Indians at Rossville.
Needing more help in translating, Evans asked that William
Mason and Henry Steinhauer join him at Rossville from the
Fort Frances mission at Lac La Pluie. In return he sent Peter
Jacobs to manage the mission post which the two men had
founded. With more help for the important work of translating
and printing, now at the height of its importance, Rossville
Mission became a primary centre of translating and publishing
in the Cree language. The books would find their way to
Indians all over northern and north-western Canada. At differ-
ent times James and Mary Evans, Henry Steinhauer, Thomas
Hassell, William Mason and his wife Sofia, and John Sinclair
worked there.

As noted, Hassell and Steinhauer were Indians who had
been well-educated in Upper Canada. Living comfortably in
both cultures and languages, their contribution to the authen-
ticity of the translation work has perhaps not been given the
prominence it deserves. There was expertise among the others
too. John Sinclair the son of a Hudson's Bay Company officer
and Cree mother, had been raised speaking both languages, but
perhaps he had a less subtle mind than either of Steinhauer or
Hassell. Sophia Mason, whose mother was Cree, worked
extensively on a translation of the Bible. Mason's translation
was considered so competent, that her name appears on the fly-
leaf, the only female missionary to be thus honoured.

If Evans made a huge impact on the north-west through his
philological work and as the region's first printer, he also made
an impact there for another, more whimsical reason. While on
a trip to York Factory in the fall of 1842, he was watching the
tinsmith at work when it came to him that a canoe made of tin
would be lighter and more durable than the traditional bark-
clad canoes of the Indians. Learning what he felt he needed to
know about tin-smithing from the tradesmen in the shop, and
inventing where necessary, Evans built himself a tin canoe, giving great amusement to the white people at York Factory.
Letitia Hargrave mentioned the canoe in a letter to Dugald
MacTavish on the 8th of September 1842. *"He has been busy
making a tin canoe all the time he has been here,"* she wrote.

"It looks very stylish but I don't know how it will paddle."

The Indians, on the other hand, were quick to see its advantages. They were immediately impressed when Evans demonstrated that, while his tin canoe could comfortably transport six men, only two were needed to carry it during portages.

Satisfied that it would serve well, Evans sailed the canoe back to Norway House with Hassell and two Indian helpers. Included in their load was printing paper, books from the Mission Society and second-hand clothing for the Indians at Rossville, sent from benefactors in England. The tin was so new that it glittered and shone in the sunlight. Wherever he went, the Indians called the canoe his Shining Island or his Island of Light. In the next four years, the Shining Island would carry Evans on his work for thousands of miles through some of the most lonely and difficult terrain in the world, proving its worth mile after mile as a light, durable, portable and capacious vessel.

Chapter Eight

$\mathscr{T}$HE NORTH-WEST WAS CHANGING. Slowly but inexorably the whole country was being opened up by the railways and by new land routes across Upper Canada, the Prairies and the West. Sensible people could see the implications this would have for the north-west's traditional way of life. At the same time, independent fur dealers were twisting the venerable Hudson's Bay Company's tail by establishing themselves in competition with the Company. Often they would bypass it to sell their furs to the highest bidder. Some trappers, tired of being beholden to the whim of the Company, were even shipping their furs south-west to the American coast for transport to Europe, instead of north to York Factory. In any case, it was obvious to all but the most blinkered Hudson's Bay Company employees, that the quantity and quality of furs was declining rapidly. The brightest of them, such as Ross, knew that their whole way of life was soon to disappear.

Aging, slowing down and beset by these problems, Governor Simpson became more arbitrary and difficult. He withdrew to Lower Fort Garry on the Red River, from where he conducted as much of the Company's business as he could, travelling less and less, Never, however, for a moment did he relinquish his autocratic hold over his fiefdom.

Evans' success in educating the Indians was the beginning of his downfall. Reluctant to be absent from Rossville and away from Evans' teaching and guidance, many Indians began to refuse to go out to their distant traplines and hunt fur for the Company. Such a development did not escape the attention of the martinet Simpson, nor was he pleased that Evans had persuaded the boatmen travelling to and from York Factory to give Sundays over to rest and worship. Simpson sent Donald Ross to Evans with an ultimatum: all situations detracting from the interest of the Company were to cease immediately.

Evans resisted. The Methodist Mission Society's contract with the Company expressly permitted him to hold services for the men and made no mention of the fact that religious observance

61

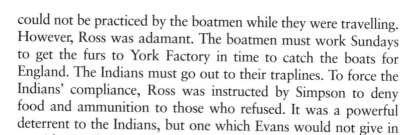

could not be practiced by the boatmen while they were travelling. However, Ross was adamant. The boatmen must work Sundays to get the furs to York Factory in time to catch the boats for England. The Indians must go out to their traplines. To force the Indians' compliance, Ross was instructed by Simpson to deny food and ammunition to those who refused. It was a powerful deterrent to the Indians, but one which Evans would not give in to without a fight.

With the company meeting being held at Lower Fort Garry instead of Norway House in 1843, Evans left with Ross and his men on a journey that would take him into the lion's den, where the 'Little Napoleon' ruled the whole of the north-west with a rod of iron from his home at the fort.

The two men had an angry confrontation. Evans inveighed against the Hudson's Bay Company and its treatment of both the boatmen and the Indians. Simpson complained that Evans owed everything to the Company and, despite this, was now obstructing its work. Simpson was unmoved by Evans' arguments, even when Evans threatened to take the matter to the Company in London and, if necessary, to Parliament and the Queen. Before he had even left Lower Fort Garry, Simpson was writing to the Mission Society in London, recommending the recall of Evans.

In the meantime, Simpson banished Evans, his family and all the missionaries from their comfortable quarters at Norway House to lesser quarters at Rossville. Although the church there was finished and in use, there were as yet no houses built for them. It was a characteristic slight by the quick-tempered Governor, but an important victory accompanied it. Simpson sent word (although not directly to Evans; by this time he preferred to deal through an intermediary, usually Ross) that the men's right to worship on Sunday without impediment was conceded.

Unfortunately, the disagreement between Evans and Simpson spilled over into Evans' relationship with Ross. The Factor was fiercely loyal to the Governor. But despite the sentiments contained in a letter written by Ross to the Hargraves at York Factory two years earlier, in which Ross had said of Evans, *"...such a man is a perfect treasure in these wilds, but*

unfortunately I am to have none of his company for the next twelve months." the rift between the two men grew and widened. Nor was the disagreeableness directed against the missionaries restricted to those at Norway House. Under duress and constraint from the Governor, acting through his underlings, former friends at other missions ceased to write to James and Mary. The rupture became so extreme that the daughter of one of Norway House's officers, a constant companion to Evans' daughter Clarissa, was withdrawn and sent to the Red River, ostensibly to school. Even Letitia Hargrave, at York Factory, aimed some ill-natured barbs at Evans and his work in sharply-worded letters to Mary.

But James and Mary Evans had suffered hardship before. They were not dismayed when, at Ross's insistence, they had to move to Rossville. Quickly they adjusted to their reduced circumstances. The houses at Rossville were built of timber, with a great stone fireplace in the middle, for cooking and heating, as well as providing light in the evening. But they hardly noticed the difference, so busy were they with teaching in the school, printing in the printing shed and tending the sick and injured.

In fact, Evans' Indian village at Rossville was a prosperous little community. He wrote to Ephraim in 1843 that there were thirty log houses for the natives at Rossville, in addition to the one in which they lived. As well, the settlement included a well, one school, a church and a variety of workshops. *"We had an excellent harvest,"* he wrote. *"Almost 1,000 bushels of potatoes, 500 bushels of grain, 100 bushels of turnips—a fair return, I think, for one year's planting in virgin soil."* The school, he noted, was prospering, too, under Thomas Hassell, with an enrollment of *"some sixty pupils."*

But, by January 1844, most of the families with whom Mary was in the habit of exchanging letters, families whom they had for the longest time considered their friends, were no longer writing to them. Many were fearful of their own equivocal position in the face of Evans' continuing feud with Simpson, whose influence over their lives was total.

The next source of trouble for Evans, which may have had more far-reaching repercussions than he could have realized at the time, was a confrontation with William Mason. Mason, finding Clarissa alone in the church, attempted to kiss her, against her wishes. Evans came in at the end of the scene in time to see Mason's crude behaviour. Immediately he told Mason that he would be removed to another posting. Mason complained to Ross, who seemingly was amused by Evans' discomfort. He wrote about the incident to Simpson at Lower Fort Garry, so that the Governor, too, could enjoy the spectacle of the missionaries falling out with one another. Simpson refused to allow Evans to transfer Mason to Lac la Ronge, even though Evans, as Superintendant of the Missions, had the authority to do so. However, for the moment the problem remained unsolved. Mason remained at Rossville, although thereafter there was a distinct and growing chilliness in his relationship with his superintendent, which would come to a head in a most ugly series of events a year or so later.

Evans went to York Factory in June 1844 to pick up supplies, only to find that the promised printing press still had not arrived from England. Naturally, suspecting that the Company was dragging its heels, he wrote to Simpson, noting that the press, promised three years earlier, had still not been delivered. He sent a similar note to the Missionary Society in London, ending with the hope that *"...the press will be aboard the company ship next Spring, without fail."*

To make Evans' life more difficult now, in the hope, no doubt, of driving both him and the mission away from Norway House, Simpson forbade the missionaries to make use of the Company's mail delivery system. Evans found this out through an embarrassing incident when he went to the Company offices one afternoon to leave mail for delivery, only to be told by the clerk that new orders had come through, denying Evans and the missionaries at Rossville the use of Company mail carriers. Evans recognized Simpson's hand in the edict, but said nothing. It was a petty slight, more an inconvenience than anything else. There were plenty of boatmen and Indians who would willingly transport his letters and packages to the independent settlement at the Red River, over which Simpson had no jurisdiction. From there, they could make their way eastwards without relying on the Hudson's Bay Company's fickle patronage.

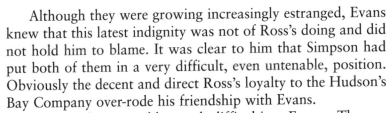

Although they were growing increasingly estranged, Evans knew that this latest indignity was not of Ross's doing and did not hold him to blame. It was clear to him that Simpson had put both of them in a very difficult, even untenable, position. Obviously the decent and direct Ross's loyalty to the Hudson's Bay Company over-rode his friendship with Evans.

Despite these troubles and difficulties, Evans, Thomas Hassell and another young Indian convert, John Oig, left on a long missionary voyage to the Chippeway in the Athabasca country in August 1844. It was to be a journey fraught with difficulty and sorrow.

As he travelled, Evans found that news of his falling-out with the Hudson's Bay Company, in the persons of Simpson and Ross, had preceded him. From Cumberland House he wrote to Mary, *"My quarrel with the governor is well known in these parts, and while all the company men are glad to see us and receive our news and gossip, they are cautious."*

They pushed on northwards towards the Athabasca country, where Hassells' Chippeway family lived, but an accident happened which cast a long and troubling shadow over Evans, both personally and professionally. On September 11, they were on the Churchill River, at the point where it met the Pine River, far north of the Saskatchewan River. Evans was in his tin canoe with Thomas Hassell and John Oig. Ducks were swimming placidly in a reed bed nearby and, mindful of their need to live as far as possible off the land, Evans reached behind himself for his gun to shoot at them. Alas, the gun went off accidentally, hitting Hassell in the back of the head and killing him instantly.

Evans and Oig returned to Norway House and recounted the story of the terrible accident. Showing the instinctive humanity for which Evans had always liked him, Ross reassured him that such accidents frequently happened and that he was in no way to blame. It was a kind gesture at a time when relations between the two were very strained, but Evans would not hide behind his position. Although Oig could vouch for what had happened, Evans knew the Indians' traditions. He insisted on making the hazardous journey to Hassell's family at their Chippeway encampment in the far north-west at Lac Isle de la Crosse, to tell them of their son's death.

This was a perilous undertaking for Evans, not only because of the long and arduous journey involved, but because he knew that according to their traditions, the Chippeway would be as entitled to kill him as to spare him. With Oig to accompany him, Evans, setting out to find Hassell's family, and did so after many long and gloomy days of travel in deserted, lonely and hostile country. Eventually they were found and captured by Chippeway Indians, taken to the Hassells' family camp and treated roughly in the process. Upon hearing the story of Hassell's death, there was an angry movement among the Indians to kill Evans in revenge. Fortunately, Hassell's mother intervened and adopted him instead, in place of her lost son. For the rest of his life, Evans supported her and Hassell's family from his meagre stipend.

While they were with the Chippeway, Evans and Oig took the opportunity to teach and preach, passing on to them the skills of reading and writing in their own language. In many respects, their sojourn there was a success, but on his return to Rossville, Evans' found that his health had been seriously impaired by his journey, while his spirits were depressed by Hassell's death. At this very low point in his life, it did not help his condition to see that nothing had improved in the relationship between the mission and the Hudson's Bay Company at Norway House. The reality was that life at Rossville had become even more difficult for him, Mary and their little band of missionaries and Indian converts. William Mason, married to a relative of Simpson's, seemed to be working both to undermine Evans to Ross and to elevate his own interests at the Rossville mission. Meanwhile the tension soon led to the Indians discussing among themselves the unpleasant situation that now existed between the missionaries.

Evans' relationship with the Hudson's Bay Company continued to deteriorate, even though he tried, as far as possible, to have nothing to do with the Factor and staff at Norway House. However, a small example will serve to illustrate the level to which Evans' stock with Simpson and Ross had fallen.

There had been a long-standing requirement that all furs taken in Hudson's Bay Company territory were to be processed and sold through the Company. In addition, pelts could not be used as currency in any form whatsoever. However, since the Indians owned very little and had no other means of showing their devotion, Evans suggested to Simpson that they be allowed to give the mission one good skin a year as a form of a tithe. Consequently, he was disappointed when Simpson refused the request out of hand, and in the most demeaning terms. The mission, Simpson haughtily pointed out, already had sufficient support from the Hudson's Bay Company and he, Evans, had no business asking for more. Indeed, at the same time that he was handing Evans off, the Governor wrote to Ross to tell him he had made arrangements for Evans to be recalled as soon as possible. In the meantime, he added, the regular stipend paid to each of the missionaries by the Hudson's Bay Company was to be reduced to a lump sum of two hundred pounds sterling annually, to cover the needs of all the Methodist missions in the north-west.

The estrangement between the former close friends, Evans and Ross, can be deduced from a letter Ross sent to Simpson at around the same time, giving him information (we might rather say gossip) about *"...this truly troublesome and restless man (Evans) which may be useful in dislodging him from the bastion which he at present so unworthily fills..."*

Simpson's refusal of his request, the diminishing of the stipends and the growing distance between himself and Ross were humiliations for Evans. In characteristic style he bore them in silence since Clarissa was getting married that summer on the 18th of August, 1845, and he did not want to create unpleasantness in advance of her celebrations.

That summer, Evans' long-awaited printing press arrived at York Factory, five years after he had been given permission to obtain it. However, once again the truculent Simpson found a new way to thwart Evans' desires. He sent word to York Factory that the press could only be transported to Norway House on the Company's York boats if Evans paid full fare for himself and cargo rates for the printing equipment. He must have known that Evans would not have been able to afford those charges. Eventually the press was taken overland to Norway House in the winter instead, a journey of fourteen days by sled and snowshoe. It arrived at the printing office

Evans had built to house it in November 1845. As he installed and set it up, planning the publication programme he was going to use the press for, Evans did not know, but he had only a year to live. That year was to be filled with heartache and suspicion.

The final problems between Evans and the Hudson's Bay Company began in January 1846, when Evans came under suspicion for impropriety with an Indian woman from Rossville, Maggie Mamenawatum, and some of the girls from the mission school. The officious and, perhaps, jealous William Mason took it upon himself, as the next senior white male member of the Rossville community, to act as investigator and judge. With a surprising lack of generosity towards his Superintendent, and with what some writers have characterized as unseemly zeal, Mason set about collecting 'evidence' in the case. He also acted as judge and jury in the hearing, which took place on February 5, 1846 in the school, where a reluctant Henry Steinhauer acted as the clerk.

The charge against Evans was that he had importuned Maggie Mamenawatum whilst at a goose-hunting camp with her some time earlier. Also it was alleged that that he had offered improper advances towards one of the young Indian girls under his care at his own house during an epidemic of illness. From this distance in time, the substance of these allegations is no longer exactly clear. However, it seems almost certain that the woman was suborned to accuse Evans as part of the effort to have him removed from Rossville. As to the young girl, he had spoken of 'loving' her as she lay ill at his own house, under Mary's care, but in the context of Christian rather than secular love. It was this that his enemies had seized upon when she had reported the words he had used, taking advantage of the ambiguity to impugn his behaviour and morals. Mason, also, seems to have played a less-than-honest and open part in the whole sorry episode, perhaps because of his relationship to Simpson and his wish to supersede Evans in the event of the latter's withdrawal from Rossville.

At the 'trial', many, both Indians and white people, spoke out for Evans, including John Oig, who was able to give Evans a thoroughly convincing alibi for the purported goose-hunting camp incident. The schoolgirls actually recanted their accusations, saying their words had been misrepresented. Even so, Mason seems to have accepted grudgingly the truth of Evans' innocence. In due course, he sent a confusing, and seemingly deliberately ambiguous report of the proceedings to Evans' superiors in London. Moreover he tried to delay Evans' own report to them, which included copies of the girls' recantations, as well as evidence favourable to him, and an account of Mason's part in the proceedings.

Despite all the evidence supporting Evans, he was recalled to London to appear before the annual Methodist conference in London, scheduled for November 1846. After journeying by canoe and then overland from Norway House, via Fort William and the Great Lakes, Evans and his wife left Boston in September. They reached London on October 2nd, after an eighteen day sea voyage.

At the meeting, Evans was entirely exonerated and Mason censured by the conference. Immediately, Evans became a much sought-after speaker at churches and meetings all over England. He would tell stories of his missionary work with the Indians of north-western Canada, and of his efforts to develop a written alphabet in their languages, as well as of the work of the Methodist missions across Canada.

Ignoring the strain that a rigorous schedule of speaking engagements put on him, Evans kept up a busy pace of preaching, teaching and public speaking. But one evening, resting after a speaking engagement at a church in the Hull area, he collapsed and died, on November 23, 1864. He was only forty-six years old.

Evans' death was recorded in two local newspapers. On November 26th, 1846, the *Eastern Counties Herald*, an east Yorkshire newspaper, noted *"The Rev. Eavins* (sic), *Wesleyan minister, late missionary from America, preached in the Wesleyan chapel, Keelby, near Caistor, in his usual spirited manner, apparently in good health, and on Monday evening, while conversing with some friends, he sunk from his chair, and instantly expired."* To which the *Hull Advertiser*, in its 'Deaths' column a day later, added, *"The corpse was brought to this town* (Hull) *by the Grimsby steamer, to the house of Mr. Lundy* (his cousin), *and interred in the preachers' vault at Waltham-street chapel."*

James Evans was a young man when he died so unexpectedly and his loss must have been keenly felt by his friends. In recognition of Evans and his work, they placed a memorial tablet in the wall of the chapel at Waltham Street, close to the vault, which read: *Sacred to the memory of the Rev. James Evans, a native of this town and son of Capt. James Evans. He laboured as a Wesleyan missionary sixteen years in British N. America, including seven years spent in the territories of the Hon. Hudson's Bay Co. among the Indians; preaching the gospel and promoting education. After addressing a Wesleyan missionary meeting at Keelby, Lincolnshire, he was suddenly called to his eternal reward. Nov. 23rd 1846, aged 46 years. This tablet was erected by his friends in Hull.*

Epilogue

IN 1954, one hundred and eight years after Evans' friends in Hull erected their memorial to him, the Waltham Street chapel in Hull was being demolished to make way for a post-war housing development. At that time, arrangements were made to have Evans' remains exhumed, cremated and shipped to Canada for burial at Norway House, where the Indians continued to revere his memory. The process was described in a May 1955 letter sent to John Avery, Superintendent of the mission at Norway House, by Dr. Frank Bailey, who was instrumental in having Evans' remains sent to Norway House.

"Just to let you know that I now (7th May) *have the ashes of James Evans, and shall be sending them to you by air as soon as I hear from the High Commissioner for Canada* (concerning documentation, customs and administrative details).

"The ashes are enclosed inside a tin box, and this in turn is enclosed inside a casket made of pitchpine from the chapel. I believe that I told you of this idea that I had, that you would like some tangible souvenir from the chapel, and the casket would prove an admirable way of making this link. Actually the chapel has been very badly damaged, first by being derelict, then by a blast during the bombing of Hull, and then by lightning. The Funeral Director who was responsible for all the operation, Mr. W. Parkin.... was very helpful in taking up my idea. But the only really suitable piece of timber in the whole chapel was one door inside the chapel, near and facing the pulpit. This door had panels of flowered pitchpine, and although it was somewhat damaged by cracks, Mr. Parkin personally has made a very good job of the casket. It was situated, strangely enough, approximately over the vault where Evans was buried, and quite close to the commemorative tablet on the wall of the church just to the left of the pulpit."

The casket containing Evans' remains was re-interred in a ceremony in June 1955, under a plain stone cairn erected by the Indians to mark his final resting place. A newspaper report of the time notes that the simple grave-side service was attended by

Major R.F. Davey, Superintendent of Education of the federal government's Indian Affairs branch; Dr. M.C. MacDonald, secretary of the Home Missionary Department of the Women's Missionary Society in Toronto; and Dr. C.H. Best, superintendent of missions for the Manitoba Conference of the United Church of Canada. *"Also present,"* the newspaper notes in the dismissive manner of the times, *"were members of the settlement's Cree population, among whom the name of James Evans is still revered."*

Bibliography

A Brief Sketch of the Life and Work of Rev. James Evans by the Rev. Dr. John MacLean, Chief Archivist of the Methodist Church of Canada. Toronto, 1896

James Evans by Lorne Pierce, The Ryerson Canadian History Readers Series. Ryerson Press, Toronto, 1926

The James Evans Story by Nan Shipley, Ryerson Press, Toronto, 1966

Trail of an Artist-Naturalist by Ernest Thompson Seton, London, 1940

The Backwoods of Canada by Catherine Parr Traill, London, 1836

Winter Studies and Summer Rambles in Canada by Anna Jameson, London, 1838

Travels through the Interior Parts of North America in the years 17766, 1767 and 1768 by Jonathan Carver, London, 1778

The Illustrated History of Canada, Ed. Craig Brown. Lester Publishing, Toronto, 1987

Reservations are for Indians by Heather Robinson. James Lewis & Samuel, Toronto 1970

The Letters of Letitia Hargrave Edited by Margaret Arnett McLeod. The Champlain Society, Toronto, 1947

In Quest of Yesterday : Haliburton Highlands Provisional County by Nila Reynolds. Provisional County of Haliburton, 1968.

The Gift to a Nation of a Written Language by The Rev. Nathaniel Burwash, LL.D. A paper read to the Royal Society of Canada, May 16, 1911. Royal Society of Canada, Toronto, 1912

Moon of Wintertime, John Webster Grant. University of Toronto Press, 1984

Notice for the meeting in Keelby, Lincolnshire, after which Evans died of a stroke.

Index

Credits

The publisher would like to thank the following people for their assistance: Dr. Robert C. Brandies, Chief Librarian, Victoria University in the University of Toronto, Rick Stapleton of the The United Church of Canada Archives; Anne Morton, Hudson's Bay Archives; Elizabeth Blight, Manitoba Culture, Heritage and Citizenship; Barbara Walkden and Derek R. Patton, Canadian Bible Society.

The Photographs

Outside front cover and half title page. The Reverend James Evans. *Credit: The Archives of The United Church of Canada, Victoria University, Toronto, Ontario. Acc. No. 76.001 P1793N.*

Page ii. Chart showing Cree syllabic alphabet. *Credit: The Archives of the United Church of Canada, Victoria University Library, Toronto, Ontario.*

Page v. Cover of 1841 Prayer Book. *Credit: Evans collection, File 11, Victoria University Library, Toronto, Ontario.*

Page vi. A page spread from the Speller and Interpreter. The illustrations are very much in the style of the 19th century wood-engraver, Thomas Bewick. *Credit: Victoria University Library, Toronto, Ontario.*

Page x. Old Stories retold for the people. No. 16. *Credit: Evans collection, Box 3, File 2, Evans Collection, Victoria University Library, Toronto, Ontario.*

Page viii. C.W. Jeffreys pen and ink sketch. *Credit: Box 3, File 3, Evans Collection, Victoria University Library, Toronto, Ontario.*

Page 17. Part of the One Hundredth Psalm in syllabic characters. *Credit: The Royal Society of Canada.*

Page 32, top. Photograph of a sketch of [Norway House]. Original print removed from circulation 77-09-29. *Credit: Cowley, FPV Coll. 6, Manitoba Culture, Heritage and Citizenship, Provincial Archives of Manitoba. No date.*

Page 32, bottom. Norway House as it appeared in 1858, from a watercolour by W.H.E. Napier. HBC Archives Photograph Collection, 1978/363-N-41/92. *Credit: Hudson's Bay Company Archives Provincial Archives of Manitoba.*

Page 33, top. "Hudson's Bay Company's Establishment. Norway House Lake Winnipeg Keewatin, November 2, 1889." by C.I. Bouchette, D.L.S. Original: 40 x 33 cm; Scale: 60 feet to 1". HBCA Map Collection

B.154/e/25 fo. 8 (N7088). *Credit: Hudson's Bay Company Archives Provincial Archives of Manitoba.*

Page 33, bottom. Norway House, June 1927. Photographer, R. Watson. HBC Archives Photograph Collection 1987/363-N-41/28c. *Credit: Hudson's Bay Company Archives Provincial Archives of Manitoba.*

Page 34. Portrait of Sir George Simpson. Black and white engraving by James Scott, 1857 after Stephen Pearce. HBCA Documentary Art Collection P-206 (N5394). *Credit: Hudson's Bay Company Archives, Provincial Archives of Manitoba.*

Page 35. Hudson's Bay Company York Boats at Norway House. HBC's 1930 calendar from a painting by Walter J. Phillips. HBCA Documentary Art Collection P-394 (N7811). *Credit: Hudson's Bay Company Archives, Provincial Archives of Manitoba.*

Page 36, top left. Pioneers in Indian Work. *Credit: The Archives of The United Church of Canada, Victoria University, Ontario. Acc. No. 93.049 P1017SN.*

Page 36, top right. Dedication of Cairn. *Credit: The Archives of The United Church of Canada, Victoria University, Toronto, Ontario. Acc. No. 93.049 P1307.*

Page 36, bottom. Certificate of Evans' ordintion as a Minister in the Welsleyan Methodist Church in British North America, given at York (Toronto) October 6th, 1833. *Credit: File 2, Evans Collection, Victoria University Library, Toronto, Ontario.*

Page 37. Statutory declaration pertaining to the matter of the translation of the English language into the Cree language and the invention of the cree syllabics. *Credit: Evans collection, Box 1, File 3, Victoria University Library, Toronto, Ontario.*

Page 74. Notice for the meeting in Keelby, Lincolnshire, after which Evans died of a stroke. *Credit: File 37, Evans Collection, Victoria University Library, Toronto, Ontario.*